DJ

DJ

The Derek Johnstone Story

Derek Johnstone
with Darrell King

BLACK & WHITE PUBLISHING

First published 2007
by Black & White Publishing Ltd
99 Giles Street, Edinburgh EH6 6BZ

1 3 5 7 9 10 8 6 4 2 07 08 09 10 11

ISBN 13: 978 1 84502 169 6
ISBN 10: 1 84502 169 X

A CIP catalogue record for this book is available from the British Library.

Typeset by Ellipsis Books Limited, Glasgow
Printed and bound by MPG Books Ltd, Bodmin, Cornwall

ACKNOWLEDGEMENTS

My thanks to Darrell King for the massive effort and hours put into writing this book – we got there, pal! – to Davie Stirling for his expert eye and to everyone at the *Evening Times*. Thanks also to Rangers FC and the supporters who I loved playing for.

I'd like to pay tribute to my dad, Ronald, and mum, Emily, for setting me on the right road, and to my stepdad, Jim, and my brothers in Dundee for backing me every step of the way.

Derek Johnstone

Many thanks to Mark Guidi for putting us on track and for all his advice and to my wife, Shannon – I could not have got there without you.

And to DJ – it was an honour and a delight.

Darrell King

DEDICATIONS

I dedicate this book to my four children, Donna, Heather, Judith and Douglas. You have always made your dad so proud.

Derek Johnstone

I'd like to dedicate my part in this book to my father, Darrell King Senior, who has been bravely fighting a brain tumour during this project. You're an inspiration, Dad.

Darrell King

CONTENTS

FOREWORD by ALLY McCOIST   xi

1   THE 1970/71 LEAGUE CUP FINAL   1

2   DEVASTATION IN DUNDEE   11

3   SIGNING FOR CELTIC   17

4   IBROX   25

5   TRAGEDY   34

6   SURGE TOWARDS SPAIN   40

7   BARCELONA   55

8   READY TO QUIT   70

9   BIG JOCK   78

10   SCOTLAND AND WORLD CUP WOE   102

11   A RELUCTANT CAPTAIN   122

12   LONDON CALLING   140

13   RETURN TO REVOLUTION   150

14   JAGGY THISTLE   168

15   ON TO THE AIRWAVES   176

16   DAVIE COOPER DEAD   186

17   DICING WITH DEATH   195

18   FAMILY VALUES   203

19   MY GREATEST RANGERS TEAMS   211

20   GREATEST EVER HURT   227

21   TRUE BLUE   231

DEREK JOHNSTONE: STATISTICS   237

FOREWORD

ALLY McCOIST

I bet every Rangers fan lucky enough to be there can still remember it. Close your eyes and you are transported back to a swaying Hampden Park and Derek Johnstone proving that dreams really do come true as he rises to head the winning goal of the 1970/71 League Cup Final against Celtic. That famous final was one of the first games I was taken to. As an eight-year-old, I was standing amongst a crowd of 106,000, watching a boy just twice my age shoot to stardom. Those of us who danced out of the famous old stadium that day were spellbound and, after what we'd just seen that day, every young Rangers fan wanted to be DJ. People claim I've had my share of scripted moments down the years but the big man steals a march on me with that one.

Derek Johnstone was my hero, closely followed by Colin Stein and one or two others. He was a phenomenon. By the age of eighteen he had added to that cup-final winner by playing a huge role in the only Rangers team ever to win a European trophy. Look at the media attention that young players are subjected to nowadays. Take Wayne Rooney, when he came through at Everton as a sixteen-year-old. Can you imagine what it would have been like for Derek had he made his start in this modern era?

Some thirteen years after that cup final, it was difficult for me to believe that here I was, sharing a dressing room with my hero. Think about it – how many players get the chance to play with the guys they idolised? It was a dream come true. We were at opposite ends of our careers. I had just arrived from St Johnstone, looking to forge a career for myself at the club I had always supported, while Derek and a few of the senior boys had been trying to kick-start the team. As Derek is the first to admit, his second spell at Ibrox never quite worked out. Rangers were going through a hard time but the spell I had with DJ was superb and he taught me a lot even in that short time.

As everyone knows, I had a pretty tough introduction to life at Ibrox. I was keen to succeed and prove myself as the main striker but, in some matches, our own supporters were so frustrated with my efforts they were advising me to be off . . . to somewhere I can't quite recall. After one particular bout of pelters, I was close to tears in the dressing room. Big DJ and Colin 'Beastie' McAdam were sitting either side of me, trying to lift my spirits.

'You'll get stick when you go out the front door but keep your head held high, throw your shoulders back and march right through them.' That was the stern message from big Derek. 'And, remember, behave with dignity. That's what Rangers players must always show – dignity.'

Sure enough, just as the boys had predicted, there was a fair crowd outside the front door at Ibrox and they were giving it to me in the neck but I took the advice I'd been given, kept my head up and walked across the road to the wee school nearby where my car was parked. As I turned left out the gates, I was pleased I'd come through unscathed. 'Dignity,' I said to myself, chuffed, 'just like DJ told me.'

Driving away, I risked a quick look to my right across

Edmiston Drive, at the group of disgruntled fans at the main door and I was just in time to see Beastie backing one fan against the wall and DJ grappling with another. And they had been banging on to *me* about dignity!

That was one of many stories from my days in the dressing room before Graeme Souness swept in and called time on many of the old faces. Derek was included in Souness's cull and I know what a sad day it was for him when he was told he had to go.

I've often wondered what it would have been like to play alongside Derek when he was in his prime. He would definitely have made goals for me – there is no question of that. He was a clever player when he operated up front and he used his body well. He was also fearless, phenomenal in the air and the perfect foil for someone who played the game the way I did. In my view, only the great John Charles – who was as good at the back as he was up front as a striker – could be compared to Derek in terms of flexibility. There are very few players who are able to play so consistently well in both positions.

Derek scored one of the best headed goals I've ever seen. It came against Wales at Hampden, just before the 1978 World Cup in Argentina and the big man sent a header into the net from the edge of the box – absolute quality. However, every time he speaks to me about that goal, he seems to be farther and farther away from the goal line when his head makes contact with the ball. In our last conversation, he was at Mount Florida train station when he headed it.

But, sadly, we never did get many opportunities to play together although that didn't stop us forming a fantastic relationship off the pitch. DJ has an infectious personality. He makes people laugh and he makes people feel good about themselves. He's a top bloke.

I had the honour of breaking his post-war league goals record. I stuck a penalty past big Packie Bonner in an Old Firm win at Ibrox and celebrated in front of the enclosure. Derek was covering the game for Radio Clyde and, before the kick-off, we had been having a bit of banter as we both knew I was closing in on the record. After scoring, I looked up to the gantry and saluted him. It wasn't one of those gestures designed to be a mickey-take or anything like that. It was a mark of respect as I had just taken a record from a legend. When I look back on my career at Rangers, that day remains very special for me.

We still share a laugh about our goal records. He says he would easily have passed my tally if he'd played as a striker throughout his career. He also says he never took penalties. I have to remind him that, for ninety per cent of the penalties I scored, I was the one who had been fouled for the penalties to be awarded.

Derek and I were both privileged to count the late, great Davie Cooper as one of our closest friends. The three of us shared some truly fantastic times. We were a wee gang, with different personalities that all clicked. We used to go to the racing a lot and we were known to have the odd night out! Derek and Coop provided me with some of the best laughs I've ever had.

Sadly, Derek and I were two of the last people to see Coop at the hospital before he tragically passed away at the age of just thirty-nine. It rocked us to lose someone so close – he was a former teammate but he was also more than that – he was a great pal.

Derek Johnstone and Davie Cooper – two Rangers legends. The one I miss dearly, the other I still treasure.

1

THE 1970/71 LEAGUE CUP FINAL

'There's six tickets, Derek – make sure your family are at Hampden tomorrow.' I heard the words but, for the first time since I'd met Willie Waddell, I was hardly listening. Only one thing occupied my mind – I was in the Ibrox boot room. Joe Craven, our kit man, guarded the place like a bank vault. In the ten weeks since I had started life as a professional footballer, I'd been in it twice. But here I was in the inner sanctum – I was transfixed.

'Thanks, Boss – I'm really looking forward to the final,' I said, absent-mindedly accepting the tickets.

Our coach, Jock Wallace, then uttered the statement that would change my life. 'I hope you are, Derek – you're playing.'

I almost laughed at him but this hulk of a man seldom treated anything to do with his beloved Rangers as an opportunity for humour. But he was at the wind-up, right? Me playing? This was Celtic, the most powerful team in the country, who, three years before, had won the European Cup and still had Scottish football by the throat. *And* it was the League Cup Final.

Sure, I knew Willie and Jock rated me – they had told me so a month before when I had made my first-team debut and scored two as we beat Cowdenbeath 5–0 – but I was only a raw kid of sixteen. Five months ago, I'd been sitting in a classroom at Linlathen Secondary, staring out the window and dreaming of life as a footballer. Now they wanted me to start against Celtic at Hampden? Yes, they did.

Neither man was in the mood to discuss the reasoning. Jock brushed past me to head into the first-team dressing room and Willie Waddell was climbing the marble staircase. 'Get a good night's sleep,' he growled over his shoulder.

'Highly unlikely,' I thought but I would never have dared say it – not to Mr Waddell.

My heart was pounding and my head was in the clouds as I pushed through the doors into Edmiston Drive. I made my way to the underground at Copland Road, which was my route back to the city and Queen Street Station where I'd get the train up to Dundee.

The club had arranged digs for me in Mount Florida but it was only a matter of weeks before homesickness set in so I was happy to endure the round trip from Dundee to Glasgow and back again every day if it meant I could go home. But, this time, the trek north was very different. In what seemed like a flash, I was back in the sprawling Dundee housing estate of Fintry.

It was hardly surprising my mum and my six brothers were bemused – I was breathless and unable to speak. When they finally got me sitting down, I swear seven pairs of eyes misted over when this lanky, shaking teenager explained what all the excitement was about. I was in the Rangers team for the League Cup Final – against Celtic.

The Johnstone household responded in style. The support was mobilised – as was a bus, named 'the DJ Special' – and plans for a family exodus to Glasgow were quickly put in place. While all this was going on, I lay upstairs on my bed, alone with my thoughts. The innocence of youth saved me from pondering the implications – such as the Rangers manager's bold decision blowing up in his face when a certain teenage centre forward froze. Instead, my mind was filled with images of me, Derek Johnstone from Dundee, scoring the winning goal and becoming an instant hero.

I was unable to carry out Willie Waddell's orders about a good night's sleep. I saw every hour on the clock as Friday night turned into Saturday morning – League Cup Final day.

The station platform was busier than normal for the 9.40 to Glasgow and so was the carriage. It was a sea of colour – red, white and blue, and green and white. This was the main line to Hampden for the northern hordes and I was right in the middle of them.

The tall kid in the suit didn't even merit a glance as the doors slammed shut, which was the signal for some good-natured banter and teasing to kick off. Had these Old Firm fans only known it, this kid was about to have a major say in the bragging rights for the return journey.

I busied myself with the newspapers to pass the time. As was tradition on Cup Final day, the *Daily Record* had asked the captains of all the other First Division teams to assess this latest Old Firm clash and give their verdicts on the outcome. Every one of them tipped Celtic. 'We'll see about that,' I said to myself. The fact Rangers had gone four years without a trophy held absolutely no relevance to me.

The pre-match meal at Ibrox was uneventful and nothing was said to me. Maybe Willie Waddell had put the word out to the other players not to fill my head with too much advice. Anyway, I didn't need any – I was ready.

The bus journey to Hampden seemed to take forever but, as

we snaked through the heaving streets and into Mount Florida, I saw it – Hampden Park. For years, I had sat at home with my brothers, as we crowded round the TV watching Cup Finals and Scotland games. I had dreamed of playing there and today that dream was within my grasp.

It was just before two o'clock when we went on to the pitch for a look around. The place looked vast – much bigger than it had done on TV. Already there were thousands at either end and the 'pleasantries' were being loudly voiced. But I was in my own world and quickly headed back down the tunnel and into the dressing room.

My locker was No. 9 and, by the time the last three or four seasoned pros had returned from the pitch, I was changed – strip on, socks pulled up, boots tied, the lot.

Jock shook his head as howls of laughter spread around the dressing room. 'Get yer fucking strip off and go and get a massage, son. Relax, for Christ's sake.'

By twenty past two, I was back at my locker – strip on, socks pulled up, boots tied again.

John Greig was the only player who said anything to me in the dressing room. Greigy *was* Rangers – he epitomised the club and still does to this day. As Celtic ruled the roost, he was hurting because we hadn't won a trophy since the Scottish Cup in May 1966. And he was hurting even more because he had been ruled out of the Cup Final with flu. But Greigy was still very much part of the day.

'Listen, son,' he said to me, 'don't look up when you get out there. There will be over 100,000 people and, if you look at them, it will hit you like a sledgehammer. Believe in yourself and play your game. You are Derek Johnstone, Derek Johnstone of Glasgow Rangers now.'

I hung on every word and nodded. John Greig was my captain and I wasn't going to let him down.

Willie Waddell left the final instructions to Jock. 'Stay in the box, son. We don't want you out on the wing trying to be fancy – just keep your arse in that box and throw yourself at every cross that comes in.'

I wasn't going to let Jock down either. The consequences of that didn't bear thinking about.

On the opposite side of the tunnel was the Celtic team. They would be led out by their captain and inspiration, Billy McNeill, and, by now, he knew he would be marking a sixteen-year-old making his Rangers debut. Just time for a back pocket to be stitched into the shorts, a perfect fit for the boy blue. But, despite all I knew about the likes of Billy McNeill and Jim Craig, I didn't give them a moment's thought. I feared nothing – apart, that is, from having to face Jock and Willie (and Greigy) if I let them down.

All Greigy's words of inspiration were to no avail as I found myself reduced to a crumbling wreck when we cleared the tunnel. The wall of noise that greeted the team was unlike anything I'd ever heard. Away to my left was a sea of blue and, to the right, a mass of green – 106,000 screaming voices.

I struggle to recall much about the start of that game. My legs may have been moving and, to the watching world, I was participating but it was a total blur for me. Celtic, I can recall, had the best of the play as the odds started edging towards the outcome everyone had predicted.

It was at 3.41 p.m. on Saturday, 24 October 1970 when my life changed. Willie Johnston gathered the ball on the right wing. I knew wee Bud was able to deliver the sweetest of crosses and, in training, we had already forged a decent understanding.

The ball seemed to hang in the air for an eternity and those final words of Jock came back to me – 'It's up to you to make the most of anything that comes into the box.' I was lucky. I could see Jim Craig had come too far forward. With Billy McNeill behind me, I had to time it right – this was my moment. The second I connected with the ball, I knew it was in. I rose between two of the best defenders in the game and powered my header downwards and into the corner of the net past the despairing keeper Evan Williams for the opening goal. As I looked up, the Rangers end behind the goal exploded and the stairways disappeared. Our support had united in sheer joy.

However, the reaction to that goal was nothing compared to the outpouring of emotion that met the final whistle. Rangers had been enveloped in misery as, across the city, their greatest rivals were winning everything but this was the day we had bitten back.

The look on the faces of the likes of Greigy and Sandy Jardine said everything as I was mobbed on the pitch by my teammates. John and Sandy were the two established guys in the team who had been through the lean times and how they were savouring this moment!

The memory of going up for that medal and witnessing the surreal sight of one half of that famous old stadium empty and the other half in dreamland will never leave me. The game went by in such a flash but that presentation took forever. And I was immersed in every moment, totally unaware that, with one movement of my head, one goal, my life was never to be the same again.

Still today, when I speak to players about cup finals, I tell them to savour every moment. In this game, you just never know if it will be your last.

In the dressing room, Willie Waddell was ecstatic but, in another example of how the great man worked, he found time to give wee Bud a right rollicking. Towards the end of the final, Bud had literally sat on the ball and this had seriously angered the boss. The wee man was told in no uncertain terms that Rangers had no right to be showboating as we'd won nothing for years.

I loved wee Bud – on the pitch and off it. He had so much ability and he had that bit of cheek in his game that made him different.

Yes, it was a great day for the club and a great day for the fans but it was only one step along the road Willie Waddell wanted to take us.

After the game, we headed back to Ibrox for a meal and, as some of the wives and families partied the night away, I sat in the corner with a Coke. It was just starting to hit me what I had achieved but I had little time to dwell on the memory. Along with the likes of Graeme Souness, I had to be on a plane in the morning as part of the Scotland Under-18 squad heading to Iceland for a European Youth Championship qualification match in Reykjavik.

I stayed the night with John Greig's uncle George. I had a great night with him and his young family and was up early doors for the journey to Glasgow Airport. When I walked into the terminal, I felt eyes on me. People looked up from their newspapers, which had my name and face emblazoned all over them, and whispered to each other. It was a good feeling but I was quickly brought back down to earth by the rest of the players and the manager of the Under-18s, Bobby Seith.

After my Hampden heroics, I thought I would be a certainty to play in Iceland. I trained with the rest of the squad and awaited confirmation. However, on the day of the game, Mr Seith called me over after breakfast.

'This is it,' I thought.

'You won't be involved tonight, Derek,' he said. 'You don't have enough experience.'

Looking back, he was probably right – after all, I had only played two games for Rangers – but, still, I could not believe what I was hearing. Not enough experience? I had just played in front of 106,000 people. 'How many of your team that night has done that, Mr Seith?'

But such was the naivety of youth. He had to think about what was best for the team and, yes, I had not played a lot of football at such a high level. I went back to my room and, I have to admit, I sulked a bit – playing was all I could think about.

The game was played and the final score was Iceland 1, Scotland 3. We headed home – and then disaster struck. As we were coming in to land at Glasgow, this horrible feeling came over me. You've all felt it – that moment when you realise you've lost something. I felt in every pocket of my suit – nothing. As I grabbed my bag from the conveyor belt and frantically started rummaging through it, the rest of the players must have wondered what the hell had got into this new kid on the block.

'Shit,' I said to myself. 'It's gone.' Just days after winning the League Cup Final for Rangers, I had lost my medal.

I grabbed a taxi and headed straight to Ibrox. I was panting as I belted up the marble staircase and battered on the door marked 'MANAGER'.

'Shit,' I said again. 'What am I going to tell the boss?' I feared he would savage me and ask me how I could have been so stupid.

But Willie Waddell, at times, had the art of surprising you with completely the opposite reaction to the one you expect. He patiently talked me through it step by step – when did you last have it, what was the name of the airline and the hotel and, a few hours later, he had traced the medal. A chambermaid had found it in one of the bedside drawers in my hotel room. Within a couple of days, it was back in my hand.

That was the thing about Willie Waddell, he helped his players in any way he could. If you gave him your all, then he would treat you like an adult. He was a fantastic man and he commanded respect from all his players but there was a line . . . God, there was a line!

He wasn't slow in sending for you and dishing out the most blistering dressing-downs, such as the one I had seen with wee Bud in the Hampden dressing room after the final. And it wasn't long before he was sending for me.

The press interest in me had exploded and a reporter had come to Ibrox to interview me after training. In those days, the press would just hang about the front reception on the off chance of a quick word with a player or two. There was no requirement to ask the club for permission to speak to players, as is the case nowadays. So I chatted away to this reporter about what the five or six days since that goal had been like and about the teams I had supported as a boy and who I liked in England. I said I loved English football and it would be great one day to be down there among the Liverpools, the Arsenals and the Man Uniteds of this world. Well, the following Sunday, I headed down to the local newsagent for the papers and the headline floored me – 'DJ WANTS TO LEAVE GERS FOR ENGLAND'. I was only in the door at Ibrox and already I had been well and truly stitched up.

Going into training on the Monday, I was scared out of my wits. 'What is the boss going to make of this?' I thought.

The call came. Willie Waddell wanted to see me in his office. I explained my side of events – it's a familiar tale these days for players, who complain all the time about being misquoted – and the manager accepted it. But he warned me, 'I don't want to see you shouting your mouth off. You scored the winner and you have a great chance, son, but you still have it all to prove.'

Grateful I hadn't received a bollocking, I slipped out the door. In the space of just over a week, I had scored against Celtic in the League Cup Final, lost my medal and been seen as touting myself in the press for a move to England. My initial feelings, as I walked up the steps at Hampden to get my hands on that trophy, had been confirmed – life had changed forever.

From the day I scored that goal, I had never had a single conversation with Evan Williams, Celtic's goalkeeper. But then, at the beginning of 2007, I walked into a pub in Balloch and I was aware of a guy in the corner who kept staring over. It was Evan. He headed over towards me and said, 'For God's sake, don't nod your head, big man. You'll make me dive over these three tables!'

We had a beer and a laugh about the final and, as we chatted, I wondered to how different my life would have been if Evan had saved that header.

2

DEVASTATION IN DUNDEE

Dad was a foreman in the Tay Bridge Jute Mills in Dundee. He was a grafter, a proud man who tried his damnedest to provide for his family. Across a period of twenty years, Ronald Johnstone had fathered seven sons with my mum Emily and the Johnstone clan was a tight unit. We were never awash with money but we got by as he battled against serious asthma.

As he endured yet another health problem, I made the journey from Fintry Primary to Dundee Royal Infirmary faithfully every night. I may have been just ten but letting my dad know he was never far from my thoughts was always so important to me. I wasn't going to let him down by not showing up, even if a game of football in the streets was calling me.

As I turned into the ward, where he had been fighting to overcome his latest horrendous breathing problems, I saw that his bed lay empty. I found a nurse and asked her where my dad had been moved.

'Haven't you spoken to your mother?' she asked.

I told her I hadn't. I had come straight from school and there had been no message left there for me.

'Well, I think you should.'

I was too young to recognise the nurse's silent commiseration. As I turned to leave, she shouted me back and thrust into my hand four half crowns (the equivalent today of 50p) that had sat on Dad's bedside cabinet. The money was for him to buy the *Evening Telegraph* when it was brought round to the wards each day. Dad loved the *Telly*, as the paper is known on Tayside. It was the only way to get the real local news and he had read my name many times in the football reports. Occasionally, there would even be a small photo – such as the time I had scored ten goals in a game for either the school or the boys' club. As he battled bravely against illness, seeing my name always cheered him up but, that night, the paper money lay unspent.

Grasping these chunky bits of silver, I headed home. When I entered the house and saw my mother and all my brothers crammed into the living room, I knew something dreadful had happened.

Looking down at my hand and seeing the money, Mum realised I had been to the hospital and had found an empty, newly made bed. 'Your dad has passed away, Derek,' she whispered, trying to force a smile through her tears, trying to lift the burden from her boys in the face of such utter tragedy. At the age of just forty-one, she had lost her husband.

I was the last person to see my forty-six-year-old dad alive. As usual, I had visited him in hospital after school the night before. His death hit me hard – I was having nightmares and struggling to sleep.

With seven sons, it was difficult for Dad to dedicate lots of time to each one individually – and grafting all the hours he did to bring in money and ensure food was always on the table made it even harder. But he saw something in me at an early age and always encouraged me. When he could, Dad would come and watch me play with my older brothers and try to pass on advice. He was never a football fanatic but he had brought us up as United fans and they were his team.

Now that he was gone, I sought solace at Tannadice, where he had taken me as a bairn. After the final whistle at one midweek game, I wanted to get home quickly and, as I was coming down the hill towards Dens Park, I had an overpowering urge to look up into the night sky. There was a bright full moon and then I saw my dad's face looking down on me. I was rooted to the spot and a warm feeling seeped through me. It was a message from my dad, telling me it was all right. The nightmares of being the last person to see him would go away; I was free to get on with my life and pursue my dreams.

That experience hardened me, even though I was only ten. It gave me the belief that he was always watching over me and that I would fulfil the ambitions I had shared with my dad as, night after night, we talked about the only thing that interested me – football.

With Dad gone, my eldest brother Ronnie became head of the family. Below him was Bobby, who was to be the major influence on my football career, and then came Ian and Billy. I was the third youngest of the seven, with Brian below me and David the baby of the bunch.

Billy was a fantastic football player. He was very similar to Charlie Cooke, the great Dundee, Chelsea and Scotland winger. Ian was also very talented. He played centre half for Broughty Athletic. One season, when I was fifteen, Broughty had a title decider against Tayport and my brothers wanted me to play. I got special dispensation and scored four as we won 5–2 to lift the league championship. I got a medal and it was a fantastic feeling to play in the same team as my brothers.

I have to say my family played a huge part in setting me

out on the road to Rangers. I thank each and every one of them for the love and support they gave me. Sure, I was the one that people talked about when the Johnstone brothers were mentioned but there was never any jealousy, no sibling rivalry – we were just not that type of family.

At school, as I progressed through the various teams, I had great help from certain PE teachers but others frowned and warned me to focus on my studies in case I didn't make it. However, that message always fell on deaf ears – failure never entered my head. Slowly but surely, the teachers at Linlathen realised I would not be swayed. Well, when I was in first year, I was already playing up front for the fourth-year team!

Dundee will always be close to me and most of my family still live up there. I go back as often as I can to see my mother and my brothers and we always have a great laugh when the clan congregates.

The city has changed a lot since I lived there. There are now far more fans leaving for Rangers and Celtic games every weekend than there were during my time. Back then, you were either United or Dundee – it was simple as that. Of course, unlike nowadays, both teams were very strong and no strangers to winning things. In those days, there was no talk of the Old Firm and, before I moved to Glasgow, I was totally oblivious to religious or any other kind of divides that would soon smack me in the face when I got there.

I remember one of my first Old Firm league games at Parkhead. I was tackled very heavily on the touchline – by which Celt I honestly don't remember – and I reacted by squaring up to the offender. As I rose to my feet, fans at the front of the stand screamed at me, 'Fuck off, you orange bastard.'

I paid no attention as I hadn't a clue what it meant but, in the dressing room after the game, I said to Jock Wallace, 'The fans were calling me an orange bastard. Surely it should be a blue bastard?'

Jock shook his head and grinned. 'Son,' he said, 'you have a lot to learn about this city.'

And how right he was. The religious tensions in Glasgow have always troubled me as I had never been party to any of that in Dundee. Yes, I was a Protestant but I was never aware of the negative impact that religious differences can have.

Glasgow has suffered terribly down through the years because of those tensions and I am glad to see things are now moving in the right direction. The Old Firm will not sort things out overnight and there will always be that nasty element and hard core that attaches itself to both Rangers and Celtic but I feel both clubs are winning the battle to eradicate the baggage that has dragged them down. I also think the atmosphere in Glasgow on the whole has improved and the city is now a great place to be out and about in.

But Dundee will always be my town. Every time I go home, the old memories return and they are still tinged with sadness that my dad did not see me pull on a Rangers jersey and become the professional footballer I had told him I would be.

My mum, however, did see me do it and, to this day, I have an overpowering love for her. She had so much heartache after losing my dad but she kept going for her boys. She could have failed to believe in me and forced me down other roads and maybe my dream would never have been realised. But, no, she was always there, holding the family together and setting an example. She had four jobs – working as a cleaner and a dinner lady and all sorts of other occupations – and then she would come home and take on job number five as a caring, loving mother to seven very different sons. Our mum is an incredible woman.

3

SIGNING FOR CELTIC

Standing 5ft 11in at the age of twelve meant it was always going to be difficult for me to stay submerged in the background. Not that I ever wanted to, of course – cockiness was part of my game.

The name Derek Johnstone was beginning to do the rounds in Dundee's footballing circles. On Saturday mornings, I would play with the school team and, in the afternoons, I would line up for Saint Francis Boys' Club – in the famous green-and-white Celtic hoops. The club was a breeding ground for young players in the city and when a much-talked-about giant striker began running amok for their under-18s at the age of just fourteen, interest in them had never been greater.

Without my dad for guidance, it was my brother Bobby who took control of my development. With his wee brother's future at stake, he was determined to get it right, even if that meant clipping my wings when I began to talk like I knew more than I actually did.

Bobby had taken me to Tannadice as a youngster and, in my eyes, there was only one team I wanted to sign for – Dundee United. They were my team – *my* United – and I dreamed of pulling on that tangerine strip and turning out in front of my hometown crowd. Sure, they were not the biggest in Scotland

and they were minnows compared to some of the teams that were hounding Bobby to get my name on those schoolboy forms that would lead to a professional contract. The list of clubs that wanted to sign me was endless. Rangers and Celtic were visitors on a weekly basis and Bobby was told that a move to either half of the Old Firm would be a formality if I wanted it. Then there was Leeds United, Chelsea, Arsenal and Aston Villa all chasing me. So Bobby tried to convince his stubborn wee brother there was a better option out there than United but this was my life and United were my world.

However, nothing could prepare me for the huge disappointment as I embarked on pre-arranged training sessions at Tannadice on Tuesday and Thursday nights with the other hopefuls. There was no training, just running around the track. I couldn't believe United were such a shambles. Here they had the best kids in the city wanting to sign for them but there was no coaching, nothing. My heart was breaking at the thought of it but there was no way I was going back. Bobby had heard how bad it was before he agreed I should go but he knew I had to find out for myself.

However, United did improve their youth system and had a lot of good young players coming through when they won the title in the early 80s under Jim McLean. Then they reared the likes of Duncan Ferguson who went on to sign for Rangers for £4 million. But, looking at the size of the city of Dundee and the catchment area, United – and Dundee, for that matter – don't seem to have a conveyor belt bringing through talented youngsters in the same was as, say, Hibs have had in recent years. That is something both clubs need to look at if they want to recapture the halcyon days.

In stark contrast to this, the next sales pitch that came our way was to lead us to the bright lights of London. The Arsenal manager Bertie Mee had travelled to Dundee in person to watch me several times and had now come in for my signature. As Bobby and I were on our way down south, He told me that this was my chance at the big time. To me, Arsenal were just another side I'd watched on *Match of the Day*, the BBC's new programme devoted to football, but the club was a member of England's footballing aristocracy and playing for them could open the door to fame and riches.

Mee's office was splendid. It had oak-panelled walls, fine furniture filled the room and the walls were adorned with pictures of famous Arsenal teams up until that day in 1968. He was a wee man with a distinctively large nose but he was warm and very friendly and he made it very clear he wanted me to sign that weekend. Initial talks took place an hour or so before Bobby and I took our seats in the directors' box at the famous Highbury Stadium for Arsenal's English First Division against Everton.

Everything was laid on for us including a tour of the stadium and dressing rooms where I found myself rubbing shoulders with the first-team players. I loved every second of Arsenal's thumping 3–0 win over Everton and, for later, a night out in the West End had been organised. We went to the London Palladium where big stars such as Les Dawson and Cliff Richard were on the bill. Here was a fourteen-year-old from Fintry living it up in the Smoke with his big brother. God, I felt like an Arsenal player already!

The next day, though, Mee got serious. He wanted me to sign and enter Arsenal's youth system right away. Bobby's enquiry about any financial offer to the family was quickly rebuffed but, even if he'd offered me £10,000 in my hand there and then, I wouldn't have signed for Arsenal. Sure, there wasn't one thing about our weekend that hadn't impressed me but leaving Dundee for London? That just wasn't for me – not yet, not at my age. Yes, there were senior Scots, such as George Graham and Ian Ure, at the club and Mee had said they would take me under their wings but how far would that go? They would maybe help me with digs and have the occasional word but the pros at big clubs can't really be bothered looking after the trainees. The thought of leaving Dundee at fourteen petrified me and Bobby knew it. So, if not Arsenal, then who?

The huge silver Mercedes that drew slowly into Findowrie Street had every curtain in the street twitching. Late on a muggy June night, the road normally filled with football-mad kids had emptied when darkness had begun to fall and one of the most influential figures in Scottish football had travelled to Dundee to meet me in person – and to shake hands on my move to Celtic.

When Jock Stein strolled into our front room, it was clear he meant business. At times, he talked as though I wasn't even there. He told Bobby, and some of my other brothers, who were hovering about, just what the plans would be for me *when* I signed for Celtic; not *if* I signed for Celtic. Bobby was not shy in coming forward. He had asked Bertie Mee at Arsenal if there would be any money on the table as a signing-on fee and now he was asking Jock Stein the same thing. 'Derek is, after all, said to be one of the hottest young players in Scotland, Mr Stein,' he said, trying to bolster his case.

Before we got our answer, one of our brothers had to be despatched to sort out a commotion in the street. Some of the natives were jumping up and down on the bonnet of Mr Stein's Merc.

Big Jock, untroubled, shuffled forward a few inches on the big comfy chair that had been set aside for him. 'This is Celtic, son,' he growled as, for the first time, he fixed his gaze firmly on me. 'You have to *want* to play for this club – view it as an honour. Do you want to play for this club?'

Bobby was back in control before I could find an answer. 'It all depends on what you are offering.'

I could sense Mr Stein was uneasy with this. But Bobby was fighting for his brother and what he felt I was worth.

Under that kind of pressure, many would have buckled. But Bobby – even though he was well aware of the stature of the man who sat before him – was unmoved.

'No, we don't do things like that,' said Mr Stein. 'You have to want to play for Celtic. We are the best team in Scotland and it should be an honour for any young man to play for us.'

It was obvious Jock Stein was desperate to sign me. He had, after all, travelled all the way to Dundee. The normal procedure was for a scout to take young hopefuls to Parkhead where they would meet the manager, shake hands, get a club tie on and have their pictures taken signing the forms.

That night, however, the Celtic manager left without the agreement he had come for. He wished the family goodnight but Bobby's appeal for more time to think things over had clearly not gone down well.

As we were beginning to debate the wisdom of not signing on Mr Stein's terms, the front door bell rang for the second time that evening. It was a face I knew well – Tommy Gray, the chief scout of Rangers.

Now, when it came to the Old Firm, I had no preference for one or the other. I knew nothing of the histories of these two Glasgow footballing superpowers – United were my passion.

Sure, I had watched them on TV and read stuff about them in the papers but I had no leaning either way and, to be honest, the collapse of my United dream was still bubbling away in my head.

Rangers had always seemed the keener of the two. Tommy Gray was never away from my matches and several times, at the side of some park or other around Dundee, he had made his pitch to Bobby and he'd also been on the phone to him. Now here he was he was in our front room. Goodness knows how he'd found out that the Celtic manager was paying me a visit but he had. Tommy's car had been parked at the opposite end of the street when Jock Stein's Mercedes pulled in and he must have been in a right old sweat seeing the manager of Rangers' fiercest rivals holed up in our living room for an hour. His manager, Davie White, had given him a mission – to deliver me to Ibrox – and he must have feared he'd failed.

He was hardly in the door before he was asking, 'Has the boy signed for Celtic?'

When Bobby shook his head, sheer relief spread across Tommy's face and he slumped into the chair that, just minutes earlier, had held Jock Stein. Now he could relax and, like his Celtic rival, he launched into the hard sell about what a 'great honour' it would be for me to sign for 'the glorious Glasgow Rangers'.

For the second time that night, Bobby popped the question. 'So, what is your club prepared to offer in terms of a signing-on fee for Derek?'

I don't know if it was the norm back then for clubs to offer money to get young players' signatures on their forms. Nowadays, if a top prospect is being pursued, I have no doubt certain cash inducements are dangled in front of their families.

But, at that time, none of the clubs on what was an extensive and wealthy list had offered me a penny.

Acknowledging her rightful place as head of the family, Tommy's answer was directed not to Bobby but to my mother. 'A thousand pounds,' he said.

There were sharp intakes of breath and then a hush descended. In 1968, your average working man was earning around £25 a week, a pint was 1/8d (8 or 9p) and a gallon of petrol was five shillings (25p). A thousand pounds was a fortune to a fourteen-year-old but, to a mother with seven sons, who had lost her husband less that five years before, it could be a godsend.

I loved my mother dearly. As I strove to be a footballer, she had supported me in every possible way. I had overheard her asking Bobby and the others if they believed I could actually make it but she never pressured me. Although I had been blessed with a talent that now had Rangers Football Club offering her a £1000 sweetener to get my name on their S-form, she loved the six others just the same as she loved me.

Rangers were the only club willing to offer any money. To my mind, it wasn't greed on our part. Bobby knew I was worth a signing-on fee and it was right that he should fight for me. As Tommy, sweating again, reluctantly headed off into the night with his form unsigned, the family had much to discuss. I knew this was my chance to give something back to my mother. She had grafted so hard for her seven sons whose ages spanned two decades. Never putting herself first, she only wanted the best for her children. Still pinned up on the wall was a letter from school about the cruise ship *Navassa*. It was offering kids from Scotland the chance to sail around Europe for a holiday and it had hurt her like hell when every one of my pals had signed up for the trip but she couldn't find the money for me to go.

The £1000 would certainly change things. I could go on the cruise and there would still be a right few quid left for Ma. Also, the idea of signing for Rangers was beginning to grow on me. Although I had absorbed every word Tommy had said, at my age, Ibrox sounded like another world. But then I said to myself, 'Derek Johnstone of Rangers – that doesn't sound half bad.'

If her sons were Mum's life, then football was mine and, that night in 1968, I decided to sign for Rangers and my adventure was about to begin. Oh and I fair enjoyed the cruise!

4

IBROX

My immediate future may have been committed to Rangers after the tug of war that had just taken place for my signature but now the hard work was to begin – now I had to prove I was worth all the fuss.

After Rangers got my signature, I had gone to watch the odd game or two but then, during the Easter holidays of 1969, there was a training camp at Ibrox for all the S-form kids. This offered the club a chance to run a close eye over the talent they had invested in. Football is no different today – youngsters can be superb in their early teens and outstanding as they hit sixteen or seventeen but many then disappear completely. Some fail to make the step-up while others find different distractions. But, as I travelled down on the train from Dundee to Glasgow's Queen Street station, I was determined to make my mark.

We had been ordered to report to Ibrox for 10 a.m. training. Ibrox – even for the most experienced of players, the very name is daunting. Few stadiums in the world can boast such history and the impressive entrance, with its the oak-panelled foyer, the two massive marble pillars and the famous marble staircase, leaves you in no doubt about that. And that was my destination as the 7.40 from Dundee slid into Queen Street. I had never been in Glasgow and, looking back, I don't know what

I had expected. A friendly face in a Rangers blazer holding a card with my name? A taxi waiting to whisk me to the club? But there was no one – just a lanky kid looking lost as Glaswegians buzzed around getting on with their everyday business.

Rangers were taking care of my digs and other arrangements when I got there so I had not a coin in my pocket. I began to walk and, as I reached what I later learned was the impressive George Square, I had a decision to make – left, right or straight ahead? I chose left. This, of course, meant that I was heading more towards Parkhead than Ibrox! Very soon, panic was setting in. I was running seriously late and I feared that, having failed to report as ordered for training, my first day as a Rangers player could also be my last.

'Someone *must* know the way to Ibrox,' I thought. I began asking folk and my requests for directions met with varied responses. Some people looked at me as though I was daft, while others, presumably not of a Rangers persuasion, bluntly told me to piss off.

You will no doubt have heard this line before but, believe me, in this instance it is absolutely true. I stumbled across a man with flashes of a red, white and blue scarf peeking out from underneath his coat.

'Mister, how do I get to Ibrox?' I pleaded.

'Practice, son,' he chuckled, 'plenty of practice.'

Such was my panic that, right then, I didn't appreciate this introduction to Glasgow humour.

Further probing brought the directions I needed and soon the long stretch of Paisley Road West lay ahead of me. I turned into Edmiston Drive and there it was – the reddish-brown, listed facade of the massive stadium dominating the skyline with

'Aye Ready' emblazoned on the wall. I was, by this time, close to tears – tears brought on by anger, frustration and fear of what might await me. As I pushed through the front doors, other S-form boys were passing me in the opposite direction. I was two-and-a-half hours late and, while I had been trekking around a strange city, training had come and gone.

The dressing room was all but deserted. The last player was buttoning his shirt and he looked at me as if I had just landed from the moon.

'Hello, stranger, where have you been?' A figure away to my left was climbing out of one of the huge baths. This, I was to discover, was the great Willie Thornton. A legendary Rangers player, he was in charge of the S-forms' training. Willie knew he had been one boy short – the much-vaunted Derek Johnstone from Dundee had failed to show up.

As a stern-faced Willie listened to my pitiful explanation, I fully expected him to order me to about-turn and get my backside back on the train to Dundee. But the great man burst into laughter. There was no problem as far as he was concerned. This was the first time a member of the Rangers management gave me a break but it wasn't to be the last.

The club compiled dossiers on all their S-forms. Many are taken on under false pretences and chase false dreams; others don't have what it takes and are released to clubs further down the pecking order and some even decide football is not for them. At fifteen and sixteen most kids believe they are the next Pele. It can be cruel to shatter such dreams but sometimes it's for the best.

A couple of months from the end of my school career in the summer of 1970, I was to learn if my own dream was still alive. I had been summoned to Ibrox to meet the manager, Willie

Waddell. It was his call on which S-forms were to be taken on as professionals. I took a deep breath before climbing the marble staircase. I pressed the buzzer outside his office and awaited my fate.

Willie Waddell always sat perched high in his chair, which allowed him to look down on his visitors. It was intended to signal clearly who was the boss but, believe me, nobody was ever in any doubt about that anyway. His specs sat low on his nose – a trademark of the man universally known as Deedle. He stared at me and began delivering his verdict. My heart was pounding so hard his words were drowned out and he had to repeat himself. 'Young Johnstone, you've done well, son. Report back here in the summer. You are signing for Glasgow Rangers.'

I spluttered some words of thanks and then I was skipping down the staircase and out the front doors on to the street. I stepped across the road on to the central reservation and turned to look at the stadium. I couldn't believe I would soon be coming here on a daily basis.

The summer of 1970 seemed a very long one. I wanted to get going, to play football. I was hungry, full of exuberance and ready to meet every challenge. I marked off every day until the time came for me to travel to Glasgow. This time I would be going there on a permanent basis. The club had arranged digs for me in Bolton Drive, Mount Florida, and I would be sharing with Derek Renton, another hopeful who was trying to battle his way into the first team.

Derek was twenty-two, six years older than me. He had me wide-eyed with stories about the reserves, but warned me it could be some time before I reached that level. 'There is a third team, Derek,' he said. 'You'll be starting off there and, if you do well, then there is an outside chance you could get an appearance as a sub in the reserves maybe towards the end of the season. If you are not knocking on the first-team door around the age of twenty-one, they will probably let you go.'

Derek was a big help to me as life was not easy in the big city. He was a good player and ended up at Hearts.

Things were going fairly well at training but, off the pitch, I was really struggling to settle. For all my height, I was quite a shy lad. I found it tough to adjust to the digs set-up. I had been reared in a bustling family environment and being away from my mother's expert care and my six brothers was a real wrench.

Although Derek did help me a lot, he was much older than me so he could go out for a few beers with his mates, while I was often stuck in the house. I had little option but to train and then go back to the digs in Mount Florida and dream. However, in many ways it was a blessing in disguise. Because I was struggling badly off the pitch, the only way to keep my head right was by performing where it mattered – under the watchful eyes of my new coaches.

There was a set routine for the youngsters at Ibrox. In the morning, there were mundane duties like cleaning boots and getting the kits laid out and then we'd do some training. We had our own dressing room separate from the first team's one – they trained across the road from us on the grass pitch at the old Albion ground and we trained on the gravel. After training, we'd have a bit of lunch and, finally, we'd have to tidy up the first-team dressing room. That was the chance for young players to wander the corridors – and I see them still doing that today – and it was my luck to walk straight into the top man at Rangers.

John Greig was an idol of mine. I was a Dundee United fan but he was the captain of Scotland and, back then, that meant he was well respected across the country. That's something that doesn't appear to be the case these days, what with Barry Ferguson getting booed at almost every away ground.

'You're Derek Johnstone from Dundee,' said Greigy, as he stopped me in my tracks.

I was so much in awe of the great man, I could hardly speak.

'This is the start of your career and I've heard a lot of good things said about you here. It's a long road, Derek, but keep your head down and work hard. Take advice, ask for advice and you could go very far.'

I thanked John for his words and, legs like jelly, headed off. Little did either of us know that, within ten weeks or so, he would be pouring champagne over me in the Hampden Park dressing room.

Despite Derek Renton's predictions, I was given a quick debut in reserve football, which was very different in those days. Today, reserve matches are used to give players coming back from injury a run-out and the development of young players is usually seen as being more important than results. But, when I made my debut for the Rangers reserves, it was not unusual for games, especially Old Firm matches, to attract crowds around the 20,000 mark.

After I scored in the first reserve match of the season, against Ayr United, I was picked to play again the following week. I was quickly making a name for myself and, with five goals in five reserve games, I was being propelled closer and closer to the first-team reckoning.

It was mid September 1970 and I had been given an unexpected day off to visit my family in Dundee. People at the club knew that staying in digs was not working out for me. They were anxious that I should feel settled – hence the surprise journey back to Fintry. The Johnstone brothers would put the smile back on my face.

I returned for training on the Friday. The reserves had a match on the Saturday and I followed my normal procedure and checked for my name posted on the squad list. It wasn't there. How could they drop me after I'd scored five goals in five games? I had been warned about the highs and the lows but so soon?

Then someone slapped me, none too gently, on the back. 'Well done, kid, you deserve it!' It was the booming voice of Jock Wallace. He saw the confusion on my face. 'You haven't looked at the other sheet, have you, kid?'

Pinned on the opposite wall was the squad for Rangers v Cowdenbeath 19 September 1970, Ibrox Stadium. And there, at the bottom of the list, in big, bold letters I saw it – 'DEREK JOHNSTONE'.

The first team had not started the season too well and there had been suggestions in the papers that Willie Waddell might try to inject some new blood. So, seven weeks after finishing school, I was in the Rangers squad along with all the exalted names. It was too good to be true.

Derek Renton drove me back to Mount Florida and he was as stunned as me. I could not stop talking about it and poor Derek must have felt like locking me in my bedroom.

There was not one doubt in my mind I would not play. My name was only on the squad list but trying telling this hyper sixteen-year-old he might not play a part in the next day's game. As it turned out, I was right – I was playing. The team read: McCloy, Jardine, Mathieson; Greig, McKinnon, MacDonald;

Henderson, Conn, Derek Johnstone, Smith, Willie Johnston. The sub was Colin Stein.

Ninety minutes later, I was in dreamland. I had scored twice, in the 14th and 57th minutes, in a 5–0 win in front of 31,000 people.

Back in the dressing room, one by one the Rangers stars I had watched on TV came to congratulate me. They were thrilled a young player had made such an impact and I felt like a king already.

That taste of first-team glory had left me wanting more but Colin Stein was still the man. He was a tremendous player and there was no way I could assume I now had a first-team berth ahead of Steiny.

However, on the Monday, I was told to report to the first team dressing room. Willie Waddell had decided I would be a useful asset to his squad. Rangers had gone four years without a trophy. Willie was desperately looking for a spark and he felt I was the very boy to provide it. But, much to my annoyance, I was to feature only sporadically over the next month or so, although I did have the amazing experience of being thrown on as a sub against the mighty Bayern Munich in front of more than 80,000 at Ibrox in the Inter-Cities Fairs Cup. That was a phenomenal experience – even though we could only draw the second leg 1–1 and we went out 2–1 on aggregate.

Within a couple of weeks of my debut against Cowdenbeath, I asked to see the boss. 'The digs are just not working out for me,' I told him. 'I would prefer to commute from Dundee.'

I knew that several players, such as Greigy and Sandy Jardine, came through on the train from Edinburgh so there seemed to be no reason I couldn't travel up and down from Dundee. But the boss was concerned about the timing. To be at Ibrox for ten o'clock training, I would need to get the 7.40 train every morning. This would get me in to Glasgow for 9.30, giving me half an hour to cross the city. I assured him this would not be a problem and so it was that Fintry became my home again. And, just as I had known it would, the return to my roots helped me no end. I was back under my mother's wing, back with the family I loved and missed so much.

Slowly but surely, I began to feel a part of the first-team dressing room. Young players are always targets for the wind-up merchants and I was no different. If you don't start to give it back, you are dead. I soon realised that and relaxed enough to allow my own personality to come out. The older pros liked that – a young upstart from Dundee with a bit of front. But they also knew I could play.

Wee Willie Henderson was the king of that dressing room – with his wise cracks and his patter, you could describe him as a latter-day Ally McCoist. I loved listening to wee Willie. He was – still is, in fact – a guy with an incredible ability to deliver one-liners and I knew I had to bite back or be mauled.

I longed for a bit more first-team action but, apart from that, life could not be better. The League Cup Final against Celtic was on the horizon and things were to change forever after that. But there was also a dark day to deal with – something I have never spoken publicly about until now.

5

TRAGEDY

The goal I scored to win the 1970/71 League Cup Final ended Rangers' barren spell of four years without a trophy and, to some extent, it also justified Willie Waddell's decision to inject some youth into the team. We had rocked Celtic – for a day, anyway – at a time when they looked invincible. They were at the height of their powers and we had stunned them by winning that cup in October but the League Championship was following a familiar pattern. Inconsistency had again affected Rangers and we were trailing our greatest rivals who, just three games into the season, had delivered a message of intent by beating us 2–0 at Parkhead with a bit to spare.

The title always looked out of our grasp. Celtic were on a run of five league victories in a row and we looked incapable of preventing them making it six. We started 1971 in disappointing fashion, going down 3–1 at Falkirk on New Year's Day, with Alfie Conn getting the goal. It was hardly perfect preparation for another game just twenty-four hours later when Celtic would stride across the city to face us at Ibrox.

Old Firm games are like no others. On any given day, no matter the form, no matter the injuries, both teams are capable of winning. That is just the nature of the fixture and it always will be. And there is always something extra special about the

Ne'erday game. But this one, on 2 January 1971, was to be remembered as the darkest day in the history of Rangers Football Club – the day when sixty-six fans lost their lives while supporting the team they loved. I have seldom spoken of that time – it is not something anyone would want to dwell on – but it is one of the most harrowing memories of my life.

It was just another Old Firm battle with 85,000 fans packed into Ibrox, the vast majority desperate to see if we could follow up the glory of October when I had scored to bring home the League Cup. The game appeared to be heading for a draw and many fans had started drifting towards the stairways, hoping for a quick exit so that they could get back to their families and continue the New Year celebrations. Then, in the 89th minute, Jimmy Johnstone scored for Celtic. The visiting fans banked behind the goal went wild and my heart sank. There is no worse feeling than losing a goal in an Old Firm game – unless that goal comes a minute from time. You just feel that all your efforts over the previous eighty-nine minutes have been for nothing, all your hopes are drained and, worst of all, there's no time left to do anything about it.

This time, though, Colin Stein had other ideas. Steiny was a tremendous predator, a top-class operator who, in today's game, would cost millions. As the game lurched into injury time, a ball came into the box and he actually barged me out of the way to send home the equaliser. There was only time to restart – Rangers 1, Celtic 1 and honours even.

We shook hands with the Celtic players and headed back to the dressing rooms, with no inkling of what was happening on Stairway 13 behind the Rangers end.

Some reports say that, after Jinky scored, many Rangers fans headed for the exits, thinking they had just witnessed another

Old Firm defeat. But, as they went down the steep stairs, the roar that greeted Steiny's equaliser erupted behind them and prompted many fans to rush back up the stairs to see what had happened.

However, the Fatal Accident Inquiry said the disaster occurred five minutes after the final whistle, when some fans stumbled on the stairway, causing crushing in front of them. Whatever the cause, it was a shocking loss of life.

As I came out of the showers, the full story was beginning to emerge. But John Greig, Willie Mathieson and Sandy Jardine, who often travelled back to Edinburgh together, had made their usual quick getaway and were already in a car taking them to Queen Street station. All three arrived home without any knowledge of what had happened and it was the same for thousands of fans who had been at the match.

In 1971, media coverage was not what it is today. There was no blanket coverage on the radio and no Sky TV to broadcast instant reaction. I think BBC Radio were covering the game but news just didn't seem to move as quickly back then. However, I was to see for myself what was unfolding. As I left the shower area, I was met by two ambulance men carrying a body into the dressing room. I could not believe what I was witnessing.

'What the hell is happening?' I asked.

'There's been a terrible accident at the back of the Rangers end,' came the reply.

I'll never forget the look on their emotion-filled ashen faces as they struggled to stay professionally detached and get on with their jobs.

I hurriedly dressed, thanking God none of my family or friends had come down from Dundee for the game. I wanted to get out the road and let these guys get on with their harrowing task.

The corridors where chaotic and I headed down the tunnel. Darkness had fallen and it was an eerie scene, as the floodlights picked out the silhouettes of people – supporters, police, medical teams, ambulance men, club officials – all going about their ghastly business.

In a corner of the pitch, bodies were lying in neat lines on the grass. 'Are those people injured? Are they all right?' I asked, tugging at a doctor as he ran past.

'Those are the dead,' he said. 'I think we have over thirty already and there are more bodies still on the stairs.'

I took a deep breath. I just could not comprehend what was happening but it was clear that I was in the way and I needed to let the professionals get on with their jobs. All I could do was head into Glasgow and get the train home to Dundee. It was a surreal journey. There were fans in the carriage, laughing and joking and totally oblivious to what had happened at the stadium they had just left.

Sixty-six people lost their lives and 120 were injured in the Ibrox Disaster on 2 January 1971. Thirty-one of the dead were teenagers and the youngest to die was a nine-year-old boy named Nigel Pickup who had travelled up from Liverpool. Five young pals from Markinch in Fife, all members of the Glenrothes Rangers Supporters Club, never made it home. Four of them lived on the same street.

We reported back to Ibrox on Monday morning to find a club in mourning. The eyes of the world were on Rangers Football Club and Willie Waddell stepped forward to carry the burden. The entire staff was called to a meeting and told that Rangers would be represented at the funeral of every fan who had died. The players would be given details and we should arrange among ourselves who was going to which funeral.

I was only seventeen and had been to one funeral in my life – my dad's, seven years previously. Over the next two weeks I think I attended fourteen funerals. It was heartbreaking – especially when you think that almost half of those who died were around my own age. We would have a cup of tea and spend some time with the families. It's hard to say if having one or two of the Rangers players there brought them any comfort but it was the least we could do.

The strain soon began to tell on Willie Waddell. He was the public face of the club and had to deal with all the press conferences and all the statements, as well as organising the club representations at the funerals.

I always remember seeing Kenny Dalglish in the aftermath of the Hillsborough Disaster, when all those Liverpool fans lost their lives. As the manager, the figurehead at Anfield and someone steeped in the Liverpool tradition, Kenny took the strain and, just as it had for the Deedle, it took its toll.

Waddell embodied the strength of Rangers then and, from the club's darkest hour, he made it his mission to rebuild Ibrox Stadium as a permanent memorial to those who had lost their lives. And, to his eternal credit, that was exactly what he did.

He traversed Europe studying the most modern stadiums in sport and, in the Westfalenstadion in Germany, home of Borussia Dortmund, I believe he found his model for the new Ibrox.

When we did get back to football, it was hard to pick up the pieces. We didn't play a game for two weeks and there was little training done as we were attending funerals across the country. We restarted against Dundee United but the club had been torn apart and it was difficult to put any importance on football.

TRAGEDY

The league title was soon gone and I think we finished fifteen points behind Celtic. But we battled to win a place in the Scottish Cup Final. Having beaten Falkirk, St Mirren and Aberdeen, a victory over Hibs in the semi-final after a replay booked our trip to Hampden. Our opponents in that 1971 final were, once again, Celtic and, in front of more than 120,000 people, I was to find my Hampden scoring touch again. My equaliser in the late stages forced a 1–1 draw and a replay four days later. This time, the crowd was down – a mere 103,000. We never really got going and Celtic won 2–1 to clinch the league and cup double and also make it six league titles in a row.

My first season at Rangers was over. I had banked a League Cup winner's medal, featured in Europe, gone through the trauma of the Ibrox Disaster and scored in the Scottish Cup Final. My tally for the season was eight goals in fourteen starts.

With Celtic having won the title, we were destined for the European Cup Winners' Cup the following season and, under the inspired leadership of Willie Waddell, we were about to rise from the depths of despair to unimagined heights.

6

SURGE TOWARDS SPAIN

Four defeats in the first eight matches; our defence of the League Cup, which had been won so dramatically, ended before it had begun; and three Old Firm defeats in the first five weeks. Could any season ever have kicked off in such disastrous fashion?

The manner of those reverses to our old foes from across the city was seriously damaging. In our attempt to retain the League Cup section, we had gone down 2–0 and 3–0 to the Parkhead side and failed to reach the quarter-finals, which was disgraceful. In the second league match of the season, we had lost 3–2 to Celtic at Ibrox, a defeat that came hard on the heels of an opening day loss at Partick Thistle.

The natives were restless and Willie Waddell knew it. He was having to tinker with the team at a time when Celtic were at the very top of their game and it was going to take something very special to recover from such a dreadful opening. OK, it might have been too much to expect a sustained challenge to Celtic over the course and distance of a League Championship and this was something the manager was quick to tell the press at the right times. He was later to be proved correct, as we lost eleven times in thirty-four First Division matches in season 71/72.

But Deedle believed Europe was an attainable dream. Tournaments involving Continental opposition had only started in 1956 and Rangers had already been in two finals, in 1961 and 1967. They had also reached the later stages of both the European Cup and the Inter-Cities Fairs Cup on several occasions. He set about building a side that could joust with the very best teams that the 1971/72 Cup Winners' Cup had to offer.

Our first foray came in mid September against the French side Stade Rennes. The first leg was to be played in France, where a style of cavalier football that was easy on the eye was beginning to emerge.

From the very off, the preparation and planning by the management team was unbelievable. Willie Waddell would fly over to watch the opposition and a dossier would be compiled on their strengths and weaknesses. A card was written up for each player in the opposing ranks. The cards detailed what the players were good at and areas where the boss felt they were vulnerable and then these cards were handed to the players' direct Rangers opponents to study. Nothing was left to chance. All the detail and preparation made it like a military operation but the manager knew it was the only way.

A solid 4–4–2 formation was to underpin our success. At times, we moved it to 5–3–2 but the boss always went with a front pairing of and Colin Stein and Willie Johnston, whose styles complemented one another's perfectly.

Willie Waddell and Jock Wallace knew that European teams liked time on the ball and our game plan, from the first whistle that night in Rennes, was very simple – Bud and Steiny would close down their back four at every opportunity. Those two ran their socks off and acted as the spearhead for a solid midfield and defence behind them.

We pressed and harried the French all night in Brittany. I looked on from the bench, impressed by the way the boss had the team playing. This new aggressive style brought so much more energy and strength to the team and everything just seemed to click into place. It took so many teams by surprise and I think it was the key to the fantastic away results we were to achieve.

Bud scored the opening goal and that gave us the perfect foothold in the game. I recall the Rennes manager had a real go at us after the match, describing the tactics as 'anti-football', but it had worked. We harried, we hustled and we tackled. We hit balls into the channels and our strikers were sensational.

Rennes hit back to make it 1–1 but we were still thoroughly delighted with the night's work. Now it was back to Ibrox with a place in the second round looking as if it could be on the cards.

Our poor start to the season in the league and the League Cup was reflected in the home crowd for the second leg. Of course, 42,000 was still a very decent turn-out but we had been shocking domestically and the fans needed some convincing that we could have a serious tilt at European success.

Before the game, the manager again told the press he believed that cups, rather than the league, would be our best chance of silverware. That probably annoyed a lot of the fans – and maybe some of the players too – but he was only being realistic.

I was again on the bench when Rennes took to the pitch for the crucial second leg. At 1–1 and with home advantage, we had the initiative and, once more, we shocked them by adopting completely different tactics from those deployed in Brittany. Before the game, the message in the dressing room had been clear – attack from the off. Rangers pummelled Rennes that night, with wave after wave of attacks. They had arrived in Glasgow sitting in a commendable second place in the French League but we overran them.

Wee Doddie, Alex MacDonald, was to be the goal hero as we booked a place in the second round and he and Bud Johnston would go on to score a number of important goals during the glorious run that took us all the way to the final.

In Alex MacDonald, Rangers had a midfielder who was years ahead of his time. Doddie would have been perfect in the modern game as he had all the attributes to cope. In my opinion, he was one of the most underrated midfielders of his generation. He was a real pocket dynamo, with an insatiable desire to win. He could go box to box, he could tackle and he scored some crucial goals – and, despite his height disadvantage, some his best were headers. And it was his goal that proved decisive as Rangers won 1–0 on the night and 2–1 on aggregate and Rennes were despatched.

As we headed into October, the second round draw brought another testing tie – Sporting Lisbon of Portugal – and, by this time, a sense of momentum was building in the dressing room despite the fact that the home fires were still not exactly burning brightly. We would never have publicly admitted that all our eggs were in the Cup Winners' Cup basket but it was undoubtedly the case.

Guys like John Greig, Sandy Jardine, Bud Johnston and Ronnie McKinnon, who all still nursed the scars of having come so close in that last-gasp final defeat to Bayern Munich in Nuremberg in 1967 were also driving us on.

More than 50,000 turned up at Ibrox for the first leg against the Portuguese cracks and, in the first half, they were treated to an exquisite exhibition of football from a Rangers team that really was beginning to find its European feet. During the first forty-five minutes, I witnessed one of the finest displays I've ever seen. We took them apart and scored three times inside half an hour through a Colin Stein double and wee Willie Henderson, who was quite simply immense. They simply could not live with his pace or his trickery.

As they trudged off the park at half-time, Sporting looked a broken side. To be honest, Rangers could have been six or seven goals up and the tie should have been over as a contest. However, inexplicably, we took our foot off the gas in the second period and the match began to change. Sporting slowly crept back in and, as many players will tell you, sometimes one of the hardest things in the game is to try to get going up through the gears again after you've dropped the pace.

With the crowd getting restless, Sporting hit back. They snatched late goals from Chico and Gomez and a tie that had seemed done and dusted in Rangers' favour at half-time, quite amazingly, finished 3–2.

After the full-time whistle had gone, the dressing room was not a place for the faint-hearted as Jock Wallace let rip. Willie Waddell might have been the manager and the man who made the big calls but it was Jock's job to dish out the rollickings and this one did not miss the mark.

'I can't argue with that first half, that was fucking brilliant,' Big Jock growled, quite calmly at first, 'but to perform like that in the second half – just what the fuck is wrong with you? We had this tie won and you've thrown it back at them. That is not good enough. You were a fucking disgrace in the second period out there and you let those fans down!'

The looks on the players' faces said it all. They knew

themselves what a poor performance it had been and, although I hadn't played, I felt just as bad.

However, this was Europe and the learning curve was not only steep but also very ruthless. Next we faced a daunting trip to Lisbon. It was to be another night not for the faint-hearted.

Our journey to Portugal was horrendous, with an air traffic control strike in London delaying us for hours. Having to hang around was the worst kind of preparation for a keyed-up team nervously approaching a game that would decide whether or not they made it into the last eight of a major European tour-nament. The rules stated that we had to be in the country where the game was being played at least twenty-four hours before kick-off and I think we just squeezed in under the time limit, much to the relief of the manager.

Portuguese teams always have a passionate support. Benfica and Sporting were the powerhouses of the country's game then and some 60,000 fans, intent on witnessing the Scots being put to the sword, packed into the José Alvalade Stadium.

An incredible night started with end-to-end action in the first half and Sporting going in at the break 2–1 ahead. We scored to make it 2–2 and the action raged on before a shocking inci-dent introduced this seventeen-year-old to the cynical side of the European game.

Ronnie McKinnon was certainly not a dirty player – in fact, he was one of the cleanest centre halves the game has produced. He would rarely give away free kicks and, against Sporting's big, tough striker Yazalde, he was having his usual effective night.

When the pair went for a fifty-fifty ball, I had a perfect view from my seat on the bench. Yazalde went over the ball and caught Ronnie just below the knee. It was a shocking tackle and Ronnie was left writhing in agony. He signalled to the bench and made a snapping gesture with his arms but we already knew his leg had gone. It later turned out to be a double fracture.

For the first time in my life I was looking the other way, hoping not to catch the manager's eye as he surveyed his bench. He knew I was capable of playing at the back but I didn't want to go on. The decision was made and Dave Smith stepped into the breach.

The injury to Ronnie seemed to galvanise the team. As the home crowd cranked up the noise, we were awesome and again went in front to lead 5–4 on aggregate. The quarter-finals beckoned but, with just four minutes left, Gomez again hit a leveller and we headed into extra time.

Willie Henderson scored what finally appeared to be the goal that would put us through but, to their credit, Sporting came back again and, with just five minutes of extra time left, found another equaliser from Perez. The tie had ended 6–6. It had been a phenomenal evening. Over the greater part of the two matches in Glasgow and Lisbon, the quality from both teams had been exceptional.

But the drama was not over. The Dutch referee decreed that each team would take five penalty kicks to decide who went into the last eight. It was chaos. Home fans had vaulted the barriers and were on the touchline and standing behind the goal. What they witnessed was Rangers scoring just one of their five penalties while Sporting scored two. Sporting keeper Damas was carried off the pitch on the shoulders of his teammates and fans.

The distraught Rangers players headed for the dressing room – we were out. But how could the European dream we craved so badly have died after so much effort? Everyone in that away dressing room was gutted but, even at this late stage, the drama was far from over.

I remember a couple of excited Scottish journalists coming in to speak to the manager. They were reminding him that UEFA had introduced new rules that season, which stated that, in the event of drawn ties, away goals would count double. The UEFA observer and the match referee were quickly tracked down and, within five minutes or so, the result had been reversed – Rangers were through.

I have never seen the atmosphere in a dressing room change so quickly. The agony had turned to ecstasy. The match had gone on so long that it was now after midnight and so the date was 4 November 1971. I had turned eighteen and hadn't even known it!

On the flight home, I had my first legal drink and what a drink it was. Rangers had made it through to the quarter-finals of the Cup Winners' Cup after one of the most dramatic nights in the club's history.

It was not all celebrations, though. Ronnie's tragic leg break was to end his season.

Following our win in Lisbon, I was about to enter the fray at the most crucial time. During most successful cup runs, there will be decisive moments, points when those involved look back and say, 'That's when I first felt we could go all the way.' Rangers' fine performance away to Torino in the first leg of the quarter-finals was, for many, to be that moment.

Given that we had already taken care of very good outfits in Rennes and Lisbon, we had travelled to Turin full of confidence and, with the brand of football we were playing, we feared no one.

In our hotel the night before our match with the on-form Italian Cup holders, the players were settling down to watch the Juventus v Wolves European tie on TV but I was taken aside by Willie Waddell. 'I have a specialist position for you tomorrow night, Derek,' the manager told me. 'I want you to play just in front of Colin [Jackson] and Dave [Smith]. We have to keep it very tight against Torino as they are an outstanding side and we need something to take back to Ibrox.'

I listened intently. I had just turned eighteen but I was ready. I think the matches I had watched from the bench had been invaluable experience. They had given me good preparation for my introduction. My only concern was that I had been focusing on what Bud and Steiny had been doing against these Continental defences. I watched their movement and studied their runs. I had felt sure that, if I was going to play, it would be up front but now here I was being asked to help bolt the back door.

Willie Waddell had studied the famous *catennacio* system – the Italian word literally means 'a door bolt' – deployed so successfully by Herrera's Inter Milan. He knew I was adaptable and now we were going out to do a job on the Italians in their own backyard.

Torino's home ground, the Comunale Stadium, was an imposing, intimidating stadium. The fans were extremely hostile, very passionate. I think most of them felt we were cannon fodder.

Torino started like demons. Roared on by their 40,000-strong crowd, they swarmed all over us. I felt the game was passing me by – this alien position was taking some getting accustomed to – but suddenly, against the run of play, Bud Johnston gave us the lead after a fine run and cross from Willie Mathieson.

The Italians were rocked. Again we had found that crucial art of scoring away from home, something that was to be a real feature of the success story. Slowly, but surely, I started to get to grips with the game.

Colin Jackson, known to all as 'Bomber', and Dave Smith were behind me. They were two solid lads with plenty of ability to deal with what was coming their way. I set about breaking up play, picking up the Torino runners from deep. It worked a treat and, although we were penned in for long spells, we had a lead and we were determined to hold on to it.

By the break, we were shattered. They had pummelled us but hadn't been able to breach our goal. 'No reason to change,' said the boss and we went out for what was to be one of the toughest forty-five minutes I ever faced.

I always remember the boss telling the press afterwards that the second half in Turin was one of the fiercest onslaughts he'd ever seen any Scottish team endure. 'And you were watching from the sidelines, boss,' I said to myself.

It was a battle of survival. If we had lost one goal, we might have been overrun. As it was, we held out until the hour mark, when Toschi scored to make it 1–1. The battering continued for the final half hour. Pulici had a goal disallowed for offside but we emerged from a torrid evening with yet another 1–1 draw, just as we had in Rennes a few months before.

Now the expectation was really building. We were ninety minutes from the semi-finals of the European Cup-Winners' Cup. After the agony of '61 and '67, the dream of making it third time lucky was very much alive. And, by now, the Rangers fans had bought into that dream. We were heading towards the end of March and we no longer had any hope of winning the league. The Scottish Cup was still a possibility and we had a quarter-final with Motherwell to be negotiated but the fans' real focus was on Europe.

A massive crowd of more than 75,000 packed into Ibrox for the second leg against Torino. With the 1–1 away leg having put us in the box seat, the scenario was identical to the one we'd faced against Rennes. But this was quality we were facing – when Torino ran out at Ibrox, they were top of Serie A and clearly Italy's form team.

Again our tactics had to be spot on and they were. Torino were restricted to few chances and we looked fairly comfortable. It was left to that man Alex MacDonald to find the priceless goal. One minute into the second half, he made a trademark run into the box and met a cross from the right. I think it came off a knee or a thigh but, whatever, the ball went into the back of the net and Ibrox went wild. When the final whistle blew, Rangers had, for the first time ever, beaten Italian opposition over two legs *and* we were in the semi-finals of the Cup-Winners' Cup.

That night we waited to find out which three teams would join us in the semis. It turned out to be Moscow Dynamo, Berlin and . . . our old foes Bayern Munich. At the time, Bayern were probably the second best side in Europe behind Dutch cracks Ajax, who were involved in a European campaign of their own which would see them win an incredible European Cup hat-trick. Bayern provided the backbone of the West Germany side that was to win the European Championship weeks later. Two years on, in 1974, that same nucleus of players helped the Germans to lift the World Cup in their homeland – and Bayern went on to complete a European Cup-winning hat-trick of their own.

The Bayern names tripped off the tongue – Sepp Maier, Franz Beckenbauer, Paul Breitner, Hans-Georg Schwarzenbeck,

Franz Roth, Uli Hoeness and Der Bomber, Gerd Müller. It was an awesome line-up and, for the third time in five years, we were about to come face-to-face.

In terms of finding out as much as we could about the semi-final opposition, trips to Berlin and Moscow would maybe have been problematic but there were no such worries about Munich. We knew every one of them was world-class.

The first leg was in the Grunwald Stadium in Munich. If we were to have any chance of reaching the final in Barcelona, then this tie had to be kept alive.

Again I was taken aside by the manager; he had another plan. 'I want you to man-mark Uli Hoeness, Derek,' Willie Waddell said. 'I have studied this Bayern team and I believe he is the man who makes them play. You have to stop him.'

'No pressure there, then', I thought, as I headed back to my hotel room to begin the planning that was required to stop one of the best players in the game.

Around 40,000 turned up for the first leg. Just as had happened in Turin, we faced an early onslaught and the outstanding Paul Breitner scored in the 23rd minute to give Munich the lead. The pressure was intense but I was beginning to get on Hoeness's nerves. I was being a nuisance – everywhere he went, I tracked him and his frustration at not having the time to pick a pass and play his team-mates in was beginning to tell.

'You are annoying him, Derek. If he wants to go for a piss in the second half, go and open the toilet door for him,' growled Jock Wallace at the break. He knew Hoeness held the key and I was stopping him using it to open those vital doors.

We would have settled for taking a one-goal defeat back to Glasgow but that knack of finding a crucial away goal was to come to our aid again. Colin Stein drove over a cross from the right and Zobel turned the ball into his own net. It was just the injection we needed and, for all that Bayern had the lion's share of the game, Maier had to make a couple of great saves from Willie Mathieson shots as we gave them plenty to think about ahead of the return game in Glasgow.

I sat shattered in the dressing room. The manager came and sat next to me and peered over those specs that were, as always, halfway down his nose. 'I gave you a job and you did it superbly. If you can play like that at this level, then you can go very far in the game, Derek.'

His words meant a lot. I was just a kid but I had my manager behind me all the way. Willie Waddell was a man who knew when to say the right thing to a player.

By now the club was at fever pitch. We stood ninety minutes away from the final and we had Bayern in the same 1–1 position that had seen us dispatch Rennes and Torino.

But first we had to face Hibs in the Scottish Cup semi-final and disaster was to strike. The game ended 1–1, meaning a replay beckoned, but we had lost John Greig to injury. Four days before the biggest match most of us had ever played in, our captain and leader was out. Again Willie Waddell had to shuffle the pack and again he decided to gamble. In the absence of Greigy, Derek Parlane, another teenager, came in for his European debut. His task, like my own, was simple – he had to take care of the great Franz Roth.

That momentous night, in front of more than 80,000 fans, was the first time Rangers had ever worn an all-blue strip and I still get goose bumps whenever I think back to it. I've been at Ibrox on many famous European nights down through the years. Fans point to the home game against Dynamo Kiev in

1986 under Graeme Souness as the best or the classic win against Leeds in the so-called 'Battle of Britain' in 1992 as the most atmospheric. But, for me, that night against Bayern Munich has never been topped. The atmosphere in the stadium was electric and it was as if every Rangers fan knew they had a role to play that was just as important as that of every player. The term 'the 12th man' has been used a lot but, that night, the Rangers fans really were like an extra man for us.

The manager left the last talk before we took to the pitch to Big Jock. 'You have come this far – don't fucking let it go now. They might be world-class stars, they might be Bayern Munich and people might think they are unbeatable – but not tonight.' It was like that speech from *Braveheart*, when Mel Gibson rides along in front of the Scots army!

We were so pumped up, so ready. When we entered the tunnel, we gazed ahead and not one of us looked at these preened, silky stars who lined up alongside us – this was to be *our* night.

The main thing you want in a home European tie is a solid start – nothing silly, no daft goals, get the ball down and settle – but within sixty seconds, we had taken the lead. Sandy Jardine sent over what can only be described as a cross-cum-shot and somehow the ball ended up in the back of the net behind that great keeper, Sepp Maier. The stadium exploded – what a start! We now led 2–1 on aggregate and the Germans had to chase the game.

Bomber Jackson and I had again been detailed to mark Müller and Hoeness and, I have to say, we blunted their threat. For all the hype surrounding them, Bayern never really got going. With what was arguably one of the finest displays ever produced by a Scottish team, we refused to allow them to.

A second goal was always going to be crucial and what a night it turned out to be for Derek Parlane! In the 23rd minute he volleyed home a Bud Johnston corner and we were two up and through to the Cup-Winners' Cup Final.

It's still difficult, after all these years, to put into words what the scenes at the end of that game were like but I'll never forget the emotion on the faces of the guys who had lost in 1967 and had felt that their one chance at glory had gone.

And so, for the third time in fourteen years, Rangers were in a European final and, *this* time, we were not coming home without the silverware.

7

BARCELONA

Colin Bomber Jackson tried one last time to turn on the ankle that was threatening to rule him out of the biggest game of his life. I looked on from the sidelines as our physiotherapist, Tommy Craig, and Willie Waddell and Jock Wallace all watched the defender battling in vain to declare himself fit. It was clear to all of us, though, that this was one battle Bomber was destined to lose. An injection sometimes worked for the kind of injury that was restricting Bomber's movement and making him the only injury doubt for the biggest match in the club's history but, much to his disappointment, no kind of shot was going to make any difference. Sadly, it was all over for him and Colin knew it.

I felt for Bomber – just like I felt for Ronnie McKinnon, who had travelled to Barcelona in the knowledge that the broken leg he had sustained against Sporting Lisbon way back in the second round would restrict him to the role of spectator.

It was Wednesday, 24 May 1972, the morning of the game, and time was racing on at our luxury hillside hotel. I waited in my room for the knock on the door and it duly came. Big Jock and Willie Waddell shuffled into my room to tell me I would be in the starting line-up. At the age of eighteen, I was to play at centre half against Moscow Dynamo in the

European Cup-Winners' Cup Final in the famous Nou Camp Stadium.

It wasn't like nowadays, when major European finals take place right at the end of the season. It had been three weeks since the season ended when we arrived in Spain on the Monday before the game to begin our final preparations. It had been three weeks of sheer hell with the management finding it hard to keep us focused. We played some friendly games but they were useless as no one wanted to get injured. Plus the Russians had the advantage of still being involved in their domestic season.

However, once we reached the last eight and saw who was left in the competition, there was a genuine belief we could go all the way. That belief galvanised us, especially when the survivors of the 1967 Cup-Winners' Cup Final recalled how painful it had been to be part of a campaign that had ended in defeat and despair. Rangers had lost in extra time to Bayern Munich in Nuremberg just a week after Celtic had triumphed over Inter Milan in Lisbon in the European Cup. As one half of Glasgow rejoiced, the other half mourned and, after five years, that pain had never really gone away.

For John Greig, Sandy Jardine and Willie Johnston – who had also been brought up on dressing-room tales of the two-leg defeat to Fiorentina in the inaugural final in 1961 – it was time to wipe the pain of that night in Germany from the memory banks. And they kicked the butt of anyone heard to voice the slightest doubt over a Rangers win. And, during the lead-up to the big game, whenever we went out for a drink in Glasgow or anywhere else for that matter, all eighteen players would be there. There was none of the cliques and factions ripping dressing rooms apart that you hear about these days.

The preparations in Spain were fantastic. All the backroom team and all the staff were there and we had been encouraged to bring wives and girlfriends – yes, we had the WAGS back then, too! Being single, I took my mum with me, as did Graham Fyfe and Bomber.

The hotel – which we had to ourselves – was fifteen miles outside the city and the camaraderie and the squad spirit were phenomenal. For those crucial three days, a special feeling came to prevail and a real bond between the players was created. There was also a whole range of emotions – fear, pride, excitement – starting to creep in.

In between the training sessions, which had been stepped up as the game edged closer, the boss allowed us just the right amount of free time around the pool to keep us relaxed. Willie Waddell appreciated we were a fairly young team. Greigy – who I think was about twenty-nine at the time – was the old head. It was vital to keep the balance right and ensure that boredom didn't set in as we edged towards this monumental fixture.

There wasn't much doubt about the team selection. If Bomber didn't make it, I always felt I would get the nod as I'd already slotted in at centre half many times. I didn't know what to say to Bomber. What words could ever console a player who has the greatest moment of his career ripped from his grasp? But, being the man he is, he wished me all the best and then he and Ronnie headed for the hotel bar.

The only other decision for the manager was choosing between Alfie Conn and Andy Penman. He went for the youth of Alfie, a choice that was to prove a complete success.

My partner in central defence was to be Dave Smith. In my opinion, Dave was one of the best sweepers the game has ever produced. He was an exceptional defender and reader of the game. He was also the fairest of players. I don't think Dave Smith was ever booked. We spoke for a while about the game and how we would play it.

'If you feel you have a chance of going early and winning the ball, then just go,' he told me. 'Don't worry about what's going on behind you and, if you miss the ball, I'll deal with it.' He was unbelievably calm and level-headed – an insurance policy that every centre half would love to have – and his words must have stuck somewhere in my mind.

Looking back on the final, as I've done countless times, it's incredible the number of times I went early and nipped the ball away from the Moscow Dynamo strikers. The reason I was able to do that was down to Dave being in his normal place behind me. He was voted Player of the Year that season.

We were supposed to have a rest in our rooms in the afternoon before the match but, just as I had been in 1970 before the League Cup Final that had propelled me into the limelight, I was climbing the walls with excitement. But, at last, it was time for us to get on the coach.

However, we had some extra 'luggage'. Ronnie and Bomber had been drowning their sorrows all afternoon and they were both pie-eyed. We had to carry them up the bus steps and into the back seat out of sight of Jock and the boss. They probably knew – nothing much ever got past them – but we thought it best to be on the safe side. Before we set off for the stadium, our crocked duo were in full song and having a rare old time so the rest of us made as much noise as possible to drown them out until the engine started and then we were off. It was hilarious. There we were, heading for a European final, and that pair were belting out the tunes at the back of the bus. But, because it gave us all such a laugh, it actually helped to us relax.

Such had been the demands on the players for tickets that we knew a massive Rangers support would be converging on Barcelona. But what we saw on the streets left even the most experienced players stunned. There were Rangers fans everywhere, on every corner, at every taxi rank. 'God,' I thought, 'Barcelona has been turned into Govan for the day.'

It seemed to take an age to get to the Nou Camp. Going up the ramp into one of the most famous stadiums in the world is something that still lives with me. It was a sea of red, white and blue and we could see the expectation and excitement on the fans' faces.

When we had trained at the stadium the day before, it had been empty – a vast sprawling bowl that would seat 100,000 people – but, as I went out for the warm-up, it seemed different somehow. Maybe it was nerves or maybe it was the empty seats, despite thousands of Rangers fans already being in place or, more likely, it was because the Nou Camp appeared strangely lop-sided. There was no away end, no swathe of Russian fans, as only 400 had been granted exit visas to travel from Moscow.

Back in the dressing room, we settled down for the final team talk from Jock and the boss.

Moscow Dynamo had shown some tremendous form to reach the final, beating the likes of Olympiakos, Red Star Belgrade and, in their semi-final, Dinamo Berlin. We knew a fair bit about them from our team meetings but there was always that element of mystery about teams from behind the Iron Curtain. In fact, Willie Waddell had endured some high jinks when he travelled to Russia to spy on them. He met brick walls at every turn and eventually had to buy a ticket to watch them in action!

They had some tremendous players but none were household names on this side of the Curtain, as Russia was still very much a closed shop to the rest of Europe. As underdogs, not many had given them a chance of beating us but we were well warned that this would be far from the formality that was being predicted by even the great Franz Beckenbauer after we had beaten his Bayern side in the semis.

As we lined up in the tunnel, the Russians in their white jerseys certainly looked the part of the steely-eyed, unblinking comrades. They hardly flinched – not even when the teams took the field and the players of both sides saw the Rangers fans all over the stadium. I think the official attendance on the night was given as around the 25,000 mark but I believe there were far more than that inside the Nou Camp. For five years, these Rangers fans and the thousands more at home had been forced to bite their tongues when it came to the tales of the number of Celtic supporters in Lisbon and their team's win over Inter Milan. Now it was our chance to give them something to answer back with in the battle for Glasgow's bragging rights.

As we lined up for the kick-off, I stared around me and wondered where my brother Bobby and the squad from Dundee were sitting. My mother was with the wives and other family members in the directors' box area but Bobby was in with the hordes somewhere.

The Rangers team that faced Moscow Dynamo in the 1972 European Cup-Winners' Cup was:

McCloy, Jardine, Mathieson, Greig, Derek Johnstone, Smith, McLean, Conn, Stein, MacDonald and Willie Johnston

And what a start we made. There were twenty-four minutes on the clock when Dave Smith created the opener for Steiny. His precision pass found the striker, who blasted a right-foot shot into the net. We couldn't have dreamed of such an opening – 1–0 up in a European final and, for all we had been warned that Moscow could play a bit, they looked like Russian rabbits caught in the headlights. We sensed they were there for the taking and we surged on. In that first period, Rangers played as well as they had done throughout the whole run.

When we scored the second, five minutes before half-time, you could imagine the blue and white ribbons already being prepared for the trophy. Again Dave Smith was involved and, this time, his long-range cross was headed into the back of the net by Bud Johnston.

'Two ahead! This is ours,' I thought.

One of the hardest tasks the management team faced as we skipped back into the Nou Camp dressing room was to get our heads out of the clouds. With a two-goal lead against a team that looked rattled, the job was half-done but Jock was prowling around in his usual fashion, barking instructions. 'Listen, this is far from fucking finished!' he yelled. 'The next goal could be crucial. So fucking keep it tight – do *not* give them a sniff.' Jock had that ability to stop everyone in their tracks. Sure, we looked a certainty but he knew football – he knew that, if the Russians got one back, some of our younger players might panic.

And it wasn't only the Soviets who had Jock worried – some Scots were giving him anxious moments, too. In their excitement, some Rangers fans had spilled on to the pitch several times in the first half. With drink playing its part, it was more high jinks than anything. Neither the police nor the match officials looked too concerned, it has to be said, but the warning signs were there. I have to admit that, if such invasions took place today, the match would be abandoned. The authorities these days would not stand back and allow fans to encroach on to the field.

As far as the Rangers players were concerned, we were focused only on winning the trophy. We assumed the police and stewards would cope with all the other distractions. How wrong we were.

The Rangers support had already started to party as we headed out for the second half, with Jock's warning ringing in our ears. Just forty-five minutes stood between Rangers and a European trophy and, just four minutes after the interval, we were 3–0 up.

Big Peter McCloy launched one of his trademark clearances. The Girvan Lighthouse, as our keeper was known, had phenomenal distance in his kicks and this one took the Russian backline completely by surprise. Wee Bud was on it in a flash and despatched the third goal to send us and the fans into raptures. Surely we could not blow it now?

Our supporters were all over the place again and, by now, the police were looking edgy. We just wanted to get the job over and done with but there were lots of stoppages and so the amount of time added on was building.

I don't know if that third goal and, more especially, the time when it was scored, turned out to be a bad thing. If it had stayed at 2–0, we would have known that a goal from them would have made it game on again and we would never have believed the final was all but over. But, looking back, perhaps that third goal did cause us to switch off and drop down the gears. The passing wasn't as crisp and we went into a comfort zone – and it almost proved fatal.

In the 59th minute, Eshtrekov pulled the first goal back and that gave the Russians fresh heart. The nerves throughout the Rangers team began to jangle and you could feel the tension building in the stands. When Makhovikov knocked home the second, the panic was palpable. We were rocked by that Eshtrekov goal and, when Makhovikov scored that second goal in the 87th minute, it looked like we might have been facing one of the biggest disasters in the history of European finals.

Since that night, I've watched just about every European final and I can think of only two where I've truly been able to empathise with the losers. The first was in 1999, when Manchester United scored twice in the last two minutes to beat Bayern Munich – ironically, in the Nou Camp – and win the Champions League. And the other was in 2005 in Istanbul, when AC Milan threw away a three-goal lead over Liverpool in the Champions League final and lost on penalties. As I looked at those stricken Bayern and Milan players, I thought, 'That could have been us in 1972.'

How close did we come to tossing it away? For a few minutes we did fall apart and I'm sure the Russians felt they could square the game. Dave Smith even had to clear one of their efforts off the line. But I'll never forget the way John Greig hauled us over the line. The thought of losing another final must have spurred the man on. As things started to slip, he screamed encouragement and gradually we got to grips with our game again.

The final two minutes felt like two hours and, before the end, we witnessed the prelude to the impending chaos. The referee blew for a foul and our fans thought it was the final whistle and on to the pitch they charged – hundreds of them.

'Shit,' I thought to myself, 'not again?'

The police managed to get them off the park but they retreated no farther than the touchline, where they waited, like sprinters poised for the gun. When the final whistle did sound, they charged from their blocks, spreading in every direction.

These fans had seen the supporters of Celtic, Ajax and Bayern Munich all take part in pitch invasions after winning European trophies – not to mention the Scotland fans who took over Wembley – and they wanted to have a memorable one of their own. But the Spanish police snapped. They drew their batons and all hell broke loose. It was a dreadful sight. This was meant to be our finest hour but it had degenerated into a violent battle, which would have serious repercussions for the club.

As the fans swarmed over the pitch, I was grabbed from behind. It was my brother Bobby who had somehow slalomed his way through the mayhem. I had the presence of mind to strip off my jersey and I told Bobby to shove it up his jumper. With the scenes around me, there was every chance none of the players would get off the park fully clothed.

It was a struggle to get through the tide of bodies to the sanctuary of the dressing rooms but at last we managed it. We hardly had time to take in what we had achieved when word came back that things had turned very nasty outside. We were told the police had things under control but there had been injuries on both sides. All of us had family or friends in the ground and we were very concerned for their safety.

A UEFA official, with a look of total disdain on his face, came into the dressing room and summoned Greigy. He was gone only a matter of minutes and, when he returned, he was carrying the European Cup-Winners' Cup.

Greigy had been taken to a small room in the bowels of the Nou Camp, where the trophy had been thrust into his hands.

We hoisted him on to our shoulders. After everything Greigy had given to the club, it was a great moment for him but none of us could hide our disappointment. As Greigy has said many times, we felt cheated. We were never given the chance to be presented with the trophy in front of our own fans. There was no opportunity to go up, one by one, hold the silverware aloft and take the acclaim. There was no lap of honour – no pictures for posterity. We were robbed of our moment. It is the only time – to my knowledge, anyway – that a team has not been presented with a European trophy in front of their own fans.

There have been claims and counter-claims about the rights and wrongs of that night in the Nou Camp. Many fans say the Spanish police over-reacted and were out of order – which seems to be a recurring theme. We never thought there was any malice in the actions of the Rangers fans but, from the players' point of view, our moment was tarnished.

Still, the champagne flowed as we clambered from the bath with our newly won silverware and it kept flowing. And, on the coach back to our hotel for the party with our families along, the inevitable singing started up. The club had made us an offer we couldn't refuse – as much champagne as we could drink. We were determined to enjoy their unusual generosity to the full.

Next morning, the scene in almost every player's room was the same. Most of the clothing had been dumped on the floor, to be left behind. In its place, suitcases and bags bulged with bottles of champagne that, for reasons of safety and silence, were wrapped up in socks and tracksuit bottoms as we loaded them on to the bus for the journey to the airport. We carried, too, our European-Cup Winners' Cup medals, clutched tightly in our hands.

When we landed at Glasgow Airport, headlines relating to our achievement screamed out from the front pages as well as the back. There was praise for the team and condemnation for our support but some papers also carried the first reports of the severe brutality of the police in Barcelona.

We headed for Ibrox Stadium, where we were to parade the trophy. We had no idea how many fans would turn out in midweek to greet us but the scenes were amazing. Some 30,000 people had filed into Ibrox. We got on the back of a coal lorry and headed around the track for the lap of honour that had been denied us in Barcelona. In front of our fans, seeing the joy on their faces, the importance of what we had accomplished hit me for the first time.

As we snaked slowly round the track, Greigy excitedly pointed out a face in the packed Rangers end to us. Aged around forty, the guy looked unremarkable – just another happy cheering supporter, his Rangers scarf knotted at his neck. But this was no ordinary fan – it was Captain Cutlass. With ten years at the club and five league championships, Bobby Shearer was a Rangers legend. As the saying goes, if you cut the man in half, he would have bled blue.

It would have been easy that day for Bobby to have arrived at the front door of Ibrox and be invited to join the official cele-brations. A few former players had done so and they gathered at the mouth of the tunnel to watch our procession. But Bobby had travelled from his home in Hamilton to share the moment not only with us but among his own. It was a moving testa-ment to his love for the club, which never wavered until his death in 2006. Bobby Shearer *was* a legend in every sense of the word – a true Ranger.

The club, though, was in serious trouble with UEFA. Our

punishment for the scenes in Barcelona was a two-year suspension from European competition. On appeal, Willie Waddell cited other high-profile pitch invasions that had gone unpunished and the suspension was reduced to one year. It was inevitable the authorities would take strong action but, for the players, it was just another slap in the face as they were denied the opportunity to defend the trophy that had been won fair and square in a long, tough campaign.

The following season, as other teams contested the Cup-Winners' Cup, our trophy, we sat at home. AC Milan beat Leeds in the 1973 final and I genuinely believe that, had we been able to compete, we would have had a good chance of winning it again. We now had a good mix of youth and experience and the knowledge we'd accumulated from beating such quality sides on the way to Spain would only have made us stronger.

Since 1972, Barcelona and the events of that night have been a constant topic in my life. I've given countless interviews and had endless conversations about it with fans and friends. Once, during a holiday to Barcelona, I went back to the Nou Camp and it was almost as stunning to be in the stands of that great arena as it was to be on its pitch. But I want to be very clear here – the Rangers team that won the 1972 European Cup-Winners' Cup has *never* been given the credit we deserve. The club had risen from the tragedy of the Ibrox Disaster to reach their finest hour and a half but we had to be content with our fifteen minutes of fame. Our achievements were swamped by the fall-out from the pitch invasion. Everyone was more concerned with what UEFA would do – what the punishment awaiting the club would be.

We had beaten Rennes, Sporting Lisbon, Torino, Bayern Munich and Moscow Dynamo to land the trophy. Every one of those teams was either at the top or very near the top of their domestic league championships in the season we played them. Munich boasted one of the most outstanding club teams ever produced. They were world class in every sense of the term.

When, in 1967, Celtic became the first British side to win the European Cup, they were rightly lauded for their success in that flagship European tournament. They were a fantastic side, with eleven top players all born within a thirty-mile radius of Glasgow. I would never claim that what Rangers achieved in 1972 outshone Celtic's defeat of Inter Milan in Lisbon but I do believe that the teams Celtic beat on the way to their victory – Zurich, Nantes, Vojvodina, Dukla Prague and then Inter in the final – were no better than the teams we beat.

Willie Waddell always maintained that our journey to Barcelona was the hardest European run any Scottish side had ever faced. You can make up your own mind. The Lisbon Lions were rightly given a place in history at Parkhead that made them icons. Celtic recognised what they had achieved and, down the years, they have laid on dinners and matches in their honour. The Barcelona team was never accorded the same respect. We've had the odd dinner but it is as if the Cup-Winners' Cup is the skeleton in the family cupboard.

I was delighted when the Rangers fans organised a number of events in 2007 to mark the thirty-fifth anniversary of our win. It was fitting that we got together again – as always, it's great to meet up with the lads. We are all getting on a bit now but the bond among us – that spirit that carried us through four rounds and the final – is still there.

As a group, we felt we would be the first of a number of Rangers sides to win European trophies but, unfortunately, it has never happened and we remain the only team in the history of the club to have achieved such success. That saddens me. Rangers have had some very good teams since then and I would have loved nothing more than to have watched a Rangers side win a European trophy. Apart from the 1992/93 season, when Walter Smith's brilliant side came within an inch of the Champions League Final, it has never looked like happening.

The rewards in Europe today are huge but they seemed like that in my day too. My first wage as a sixteen-year-old at Rangers was £30 a week. When I ran out at the Nou Camp I was on £90 a week plus bonus, which normally took my wages up to £150. But my win bonus for the game in Barcelona had been sorted out between Greigy and the club and we were paid £1500 each. So I walked away with ten times my weekly wage in cash and I thought I was a millionaire. I would check my bank book every couple of days to make sure that the zeros were all still in the right place.

Now, looking back, I'd have swapped the money for a different outcome. The feeling of being denied our moment still hurts a bit, even after all these years. But, every day, I can reach up and touch the winner's medal that always hangs on the chain around my neck. That is something that can never be taken from me.

8

READY TO QUIT

'DJ Goes AWOL!' That's what the newspaper headlines screamed across Scotland in the summer of 1972 as they reported on the exploits of a big, daft laddie from Dundee who, if he wasn't careful, could have been heading into football oblivion.

I was suffering my personal fall-out from the high of Barcelona. The League Cup Final of 1970 may have made my name but being part of only the second Scottish team to win a European trophy was something else. The unwanted baggage it attracted was unbelievable. Everyone at Rangers was under a media microscope on a daily basis as the knock-on effects from what happened in Spain and the impending UEFA punishment ensured we remained front-page news.

I was finding it increasingly hard to stay afloat in the Glasgow goldfish bowl. There had already been a string of stories about me after my League Cup Final display against Celtic. Most of it was positive, apart from the one naughty piece of spin that suggested I wanted to leave Ibrox to play in England. At eighteen, I was now a Cup Winners' Cup hero – and a magnet for headlines and people sniffing around my private life. That side of football life has always bothered me. I know it comes with the territory but I find much of the stuff written in the news pages out of order.

Unfortunately, I set about providing the tabloids with just the kind of stories they lapped up. I needed an escape and where better for an impressionable teenager with a few quid in his pocket than London? My journey to the Big Smoke with my brother Bobby for talks with Arsenal earlier in my career had left me with a taste for the place. It's easy to get lost in London and that summer I wanted to sink into the background.

I went down with my pal Harry. A mate of ours, Ian Brittain, was playing for Chelsea and he had arranged a week's digs for me and Harry at a house in Clapham that belonged to one of his friends. 'Great,' I thought, 'a few days away from the pressures of Rangers and Glasgow.'

Pre-season training was just ten days away but a week in London would give me time to clear my head and I could still have three days back in Dundee before the new campaign got underway. The Deedle, Willie Waddell, had moved upstairs after Barcelona and Jock Wallace was now the Rangers manager. I hadn't heard from Jock but I knew the rules. I had ten days before reporting back at the club.

The family we stayed with were great. They were all Chelsea daft and there was the added attraction of a good-looking daughter. Janice was a stunning young lady and it wasn't long before the Johnstone charms were working their magic. Love was very much in the air.

For the first time in two years, I could be myself away from the glare. That week was one of the best of my life. We did the sights, took in some films, went out for a few drinks and joined in the sing-songs in the local pubs. My head was spinning. I was young, I was in love – or so I thought.

But the weeks of pent-up emotions were beginning to take their toll. Here I was, one of the most talked-about young players of my time, and I began thinking that what I really wanted was to quit football! Did I want to go back to Rangers? Was football really for me?

I decided I had had enough. With a few quid in my pocket, I could get a job in London. That would be easy. Football had propelled me into a place where I didn't feel comfortable any more and I wanted out.

The hours convincing myself I was quitting soon became days and my deadline for being back in Scotland had come and gone. I had failed to appear for training on Big Jock's first official day in charge and, up the road, those headlines screamed 'AWOL'.

I recall it was a Sunday night and Harry and I were with Janice and her family in the wee workingmen's pub in Clapham that had become our local. I was unaware of the mayhem unfolding back home – no mobile phones back then – and the press calls to my mother and to Rangers seeking my where-abouts.

As I was giving the barman our drinks order – 'Pint of bitter, gin and tonic, Sweetheart stout and a pint of lager for me, please' – the word 'please' was hardly out of my mouth when a booming voice over my left shoulder roared, 'And I'll have a half.' I didn't need to turn around to see who it was. I could hear chairs hurriedly being moved aside to allow a 6ft 4in gruff Scotsman close in on his target.

Jock Wallace didn't take kindly to being messed around and I was messing him around big-time. It was like a scene from the OK Corral, only Big Jock didn't need any deputies.

'Fuck me,' I thought, 'he's going to batter me right here and now in front of all these people.'

Jock joined me at the bar. Without a word, he picked up his

half and downed it in one go. He was sweating slightly and I hoped it was caused by the muggy London evening, rather than a rising temper.

'You'll be on that plane first thing tomorrow morning and back at Ibrox, right, son?' It was said almost in a whisper.

'Yes, boss,' was all I could manage to say in reply.

With that, the new manager of Glasgow Rangers turned and walked straight out the pub into the Clapham night and I was able to breathe for the first time in what seemed like minutes.

I couldn't believe Jock had tracked me down. Back at the digs, I phoned my mother in Dundee and asked if she had been Jock's informant but she said she had only told him I was somewhere in London. Whoever Jock had got his information from didn't matter – I had been caught bang to rights and now I had to go back and face the music.

Next day, as ordered, I reported to Ibrox. By the time I got there, it was late in the afternoon and the first team had gone for the day. Word awaited me that Jock Wallace wanted to see me in the manager's office at the head of the marble staircase. It was strange to see Jock behind a desk. He was a tracksuit manager – a coach in every sense of the word – but now he had other duties under his remit as Rangers manager and on today's agenda was meting out discipline on the errant young star he had ambushed in London the day before.

'Listen, son,' he said, calmly but with feeling, 'I know it's not been easy for you and you just want a normal life but you can never have that life again. You need to think about your career now. You have the talent to be a top player and that's why I came to get you yesterday. There is huge pressure attached to this club and you need to be able to handle it – be a man. I am here to help you whenever I can but you need to help yourself and you can never show Rangers that lack of respect again.'

By now, he was on his feet and coming around the desk. For the first time since I'd known him, I wondered if Jock Wallace was going soft. 'I'm really sorry, boss, it will never happen again. I am totally committed to Rangers and to you.'

Thinking it was all over, I turned to reach for the door handle, only to experience for the first time the infamous clip around the ear. Did I say clip? It was a full-blooded back-hander and it thudded into the side of my head, making my ears ring. Here, then, was the real Jock Wallace. Of course, nowadays, that would constitute assault but then it was common for managers to discipline players in this way.

'Get into your gear and get on to that fucking track and run your balls off – you are miles behind the rest,' he roared. 'Oh and you are also fined two weeks' wages *and* you'll be staying behind when we leave for Sweden pre-season. That is my decision, Derek.'

I couldn't argue – if you were smart, you wouldn't. Jock Wallace had pulled me back from the brink and I saw, there and then, what Rangers and every one of his players meant to him. He was a massive influence on my career.

That day, I learned that what I had achieved so far – and it was a lot – was history. Sure, we had just won a European trophy and written our names into the history books but time never stands still at a big club like Rangers and Jock knew that. With success comes expectation and that's what Jock set about ramming home to every player that summer.

I've never seen a man motivate players the way he did. He knew exactly how to deal with each individual. The great managers all have that knack. You cannot treat all the players in the same way – you need to know who needs a kick up the backside and who needs a cuddle.

Other examples of Jock's man-management – such as the times he would give players one of his clips – were designed to shock. Given the power players at many clubs now seem to have, he would probably be sacked if he tried that today but he knew what made every player in that Rangers dressing room tick. Sir Alex Ferguson at Manchester United was the same. Fergie knew, for example, that, to get the best out of David Beckham, he couldn't treat him in the same harsh way as he treated Roy Keane – a gentler approach was required when it came to Becks.

At Rangers today, Walter Smith has that same quality. During the nine-in-a-row run of the '90s, he had to deal with all manner of players – players of various nationalities and with different personalities – but he man-managed. The biggest compliment I could pay Walter is that he is like Jock in many ways. They both loved Rangers and they had the club in their blood, which meant they gained the unwavering respect of every player.

Had Jock Wallace been manager of Scotland and been looking on as Rangers toiled, then he would have gone back to Ibrox to help just as Walter did when he took over from Paul Le Guen.

How many of today's managers would jump on a plane and track down a player to a pub in London and give them another chance? These days, even if they did, they would have a P45 to hand out instead of words of wisdom. But Jock knew what I was going through. When I saw what was happening to the likes of Wayne Rooney, under enormous pressure at eighteen, and even Michael Owen, when he came through at Liverpool at such a young age, I could empathise totally.

OK, I wasn't getting the same financial rewards – I had a grand left of my Barcelona bonus on that trip to London and felt still like a millionaire! – but it's impossible for any young player to deal with all the side issues by himself and today the media desire to invade players' private lives has grown to insatiable levels.

I would have gone through with my decision to quit football that summer if Jock hadn't come to London. Maybe my head was just up my arse, maybe it was my first real experience with a female, who knows? But I was ready to do it. No matter the career I had in front of me, no matter the reputation I was forging for myself and no matter what I had achieved by the age of eighteen, I wanted out. And, anyway, if I had shown the club just one more example of disrespect, then I would have been finished at Rangers.

That night Jock saved my career and, looking back, I have no doubts about that. I would have walked away from football if Jock hadn't come to London.

Many years after my career had finished, I was speaking at a sportsmen's dinner and Jock was in the audience. We had a few drinks afterwards and chatted about old times and, inevitably, our meeting in that pub in Clapham came up. 'Tell me this, boss: how did you find me that time in London?' I asked.

'I knew you were in London, son. I went around six or seven pubs in the area where I knew you were staying and I didn't give up until I found you. You were acting like a big, daft laddie and I didn't want you to throw your career away.'

'But who told you where in London I was? It's a big place, boss.'

Jock smiled. 'It was your mother – she told me you were in

Clapham. And, if you say a word to her after all these years, I'll give you a bigger fucking slap than the one you got in my office when you came back.'

I have never mentioned it to my mother.

9

BIG JOCK

Searing pains arrowed up and down my legs with every stride and sweat formed rivulets from every pore the sand had failed to clog. Around me, seasoned professionals were bent double, with their breakfasts deposited on the dunes in front of them. Welcome to pre-season training Jock Wallace style – welcome to the hell that was Gullane.

A new era began at Ibrox when Willie Waddell moved upstairs to become General Manager in the wake of our magnificent Cup Winners' Cup success in Barcelona and its condemnatory fall-out. His trusted lieutenant, Big Jock, had taken over the manager's tracksuit and he wasted no time in making his mark.

Since his mission to London to lay things on the line for me, we had started to form a good relationship and I was determined to give him everything I had, even if I was struggling to shake off the excesses of a summer that had seen me contemplate my future in the game.

The players had the utmost respect for this hulk of a man. We were delighted he had been appointed after the Deedle's decision to move upstairs.

Jock was a no-nonsense coach, a real man's man, and he loved Rangers with an unwavering passion I've seldom encountered. From the moment he took over, there were no grey areas.

He demanded the best of every player, every day, and he demanded we respect the badge on the jersey. Rangers was everything – the individual came a poor second.

For me, his major quality was his honesty. If Jock Wallace had something to say to a player, he would do so straight to his face. If you were slacking in training, if you hadn't performed the way he expected, you were told in no uncertain terms. And, as I've said, he thought nothing of giving you a belt around the lug and there was never a word back.

Sure, there was the fear factor with him but there was also massive respect. To me, Jock is up there with the top managers the game has ever produced – Shankly, Stein, Paisley and Busby – but even they would have shared the look of bewilderment on our faces when Jock announced our preparations for the 1972/73 season would include a one-day trip to a place called Gullane on the east coast of Scotland. That bizarre session on the beach was so far removed from the accepted norm of pre-season training that it sent a clear message that Jock Wallace would do things his way.

Jock believed players who had to deal with the rigours of a Scottish domestic season, plus European and international matches, had to be super-fit. And he believed pounding the dunes would work muscles we never knew we had and set us up for the rigours of pre-season training.

Naturally, the press whipped up a sand storm. The jokes came thick and fast about this new method of training, some even suggesting we would never see a football until the first match of the season, such was Jock's obsession with fitness. But the physical side of the game meant everything to him. He wanted us to be the fittest, sharpest and hungriest team in the land.

I had never seen such scenes as heralded our first trip to Gullane. We were falling headlong all over the place as we tried to pound our way through sand that was soft in some areas, yet firm in others. Our feet just kept sinking and, all the while, big Jock, stopwatch in hand, was growling menacingly at anyone who dared pause for breath.

There were three poles placed between dunes and beach – one at the bottom, one in the middle, one at the top. We were to run in shuttles, from the starting point to the first pole and back, maybe three or four times and then to the middle and back and so on until we'd been to the top pole.

Sandy Jardine and Alex MacDonald were the fittest guys at the club and they went first. We soon worked out that the trick was to try to run in the footprints they had created. Ahead of me in the queue was big Peter McCloy – size thirteens and all! – so, thanks to his huge feet making the stride pattern easier for me, I actually had a less gruelling time of it than most of the others.

A lot of the guys in the team were already very fit but just about everyone ended up being physically sick at Gullane. It was agony, sheer hell. But Jock knew exactly what he was doing. He had called in Tom Paterson, an expert in fitness and sprint coaching, and Tom pulled off the impossible with Sandy Jardine. Sandy was one of the quickest players I've ever seen but the double sessions at Gullane and the specialist work with Tom actually made him faster and his endurance also improved.

It was an amazing pre-season. We lived in fear of whatever torture Jock and Tom would dream up next. Tom was some guy. He would whip up a drink that consisted of raw eggs, milk and sugar, and we would all have to sink it for extra energy. Then, before we had put on our kit, he would line us up and turn the cold hose on us. And, as we shivered away, he would rub whisky into our hair to freshen us up! I think he went through two or three bottles a week. This sometimes went on just before matches too so, as we lined up in the tunnel stinking of booze, the opposition must have thought we were half-cut.

Following my adventures in London, Jock had fined me and seriously chastised me but we had cleared the air and he was never a man to hold grudges. He realised I was still only eighteen and a lot had already happened in my life at Rangers but it was made perfectly clear what was expected of me. Celtic had been the dominant force in Scottish football for several seasons and it had been a long time since Rangers had won the title. Not surprisingly, this irked Jock and he wanted to be the man who turned things around.

Every day, he made it clear that he would carry no passengers. I have never seen a man with such passion. At times he could be ferocious but at others, depending on which player he was dealing with, he said exactly the right thing. I felt he liked me and I knew that he rated me but he cut me no slack just because I was a young player. I had to deliver the same performances and commitment as the senior pros.

So it was a supremely fit and well-motivated Rangers squad that embarked on our first season after the ultimate high of winning the Cup Winners' Cup. There was to be no proper European campaign, of course. That was our punishment for the trouble in the Nou Camp but at least the two-year UEFA ban had been cut in half on appeal.

We did, however, have the thought of playing against the mighty Ajax in the embryonic Super Cup to look forward to. Willie Waddell had been the architect of Super Cup. The idea was to have the winners of the European Cup and the holders of the Cup Winners' Cup play each other.

Facing the Dutch masters was a prospect to relish but, with no other competitive action on the Continent, domestic matters were very much to the fore. The season started in the worst possible fashion – three defeats in the first five league games, including a 3–1 reverse to Celtic in the opening Old Firm clash of the campaign.

The League Cup opened the season back then and our section was kind to us. With ties against Ayr United, St Mirren and Clydebank we won five games and lost just one to be top of our group. But Jock was livid with our league form. He would tear strips off the players after games and then double our training sessions.

Celtic, pursuing eight league titles in a row, were not conceding many points and we were already falling away badly. My own league form was poor. The goals had dried up and it was agreed I should go back to my more favoured position in defence. Derek Parlane formed the new attack with Alfie Conn and, almost instantly, things started to improve. It was the first big team change Jock had made and he got it bang on.

We progressed to a League Cup semi-final against Hibs but, without the injured John Greig, we went down 1–0 after a disappointing display.

The league challenge, however, was now very much alive. We beat Celtic 2–1 at Ibrox just after New Year and that gave us the platform to go into the Super Cup match against Ajax in mid January in high spirits. That Ajax side was one of the finest the world has ever had the joy to witness. They were immense and the king himself, Johan Cruyff, was their captain.

A crowd of more than 58,000 packed into Ibrox for the first

Me as a two-year-old toddler at our back door in Fintry

Showing off the trophies with my Scottish Schoolboys pal Charlie Morgan

The Johnstone clan – (at the back, left to right) Billy, me in my Schoolboys cap, Ian, Bobby and Ronnie and (at the front, left to right) David, my niece Lynne and Brian

The goal that made me! Leaping between Celtic's no. 5, Billy McNeill, and their no. 2, Jim Craig, to head home the 1970 League Cup Final winner against Celtic

Sombre times – some of the Rangers players and I attend the funeral of one of the fans who died in the tragic Ibrox Disaster of January 1971

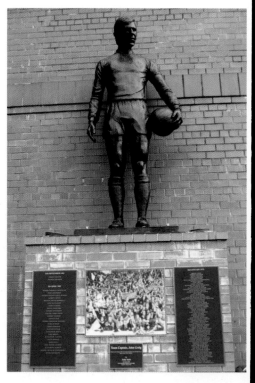

The statue of John Greig outside Ibrox that was erected in tribute to the sixty-six Rangers supporters who lost their lives that day in 1971

Alex MacDonald leads us off after the stunning 2–0 semi-final win in the Cup Winners' Cup over Bayern Munich at Ibrox in April 1972

Willie Johnstone celebrating one of the two goals he scored against Moscow Dynamo in Barcelona when Rangers won the European Cup Winners' Cup in May 1972

In the bath at Barcelona with Tam McLean, Colin Stein and Dave Smith after our 3–2 win over Moscow Dynamo to win the European Cup Winners' Cup in 1972

The squad that won the European Cup winners' Cup in 1972, with their manager, coaches and backroom staff

The 'Barcelona Bears' on the pitch at Ibrox as we celebrate the thirtieth anniversary of winning the European Cup Winners' Cup with the fans

The guys look on as I sample the rigours of training on the sands at Gullane for the first time in the summer of 1972

Jimmy 'Jinky' Johnstone skins his namesake to score the only goal in a September 1973 Old Firm clash at Ibrox

Tam 'Jaws' Forsyth scores one of the most famous goals in Scottish Cup history as we beat Celtic 3–2 in the 1973 final at Hampden

The look on Greigy's face says it all as a barren period of eleven years without Rangers winning a championship title comes to an end at Easter Road in 1975

Out-jumping Hearts' Alan Anderson as we win the 1976 Scottish Cup Final 3–1 to clinch the treble

Stuart Kennedy and I protest about referee Bob Valentine's decision to award Celtic a penalty in the 1977 Scottish Cup final at Hampden

Big Jock starts the party as we clinch another Treble by beating Aberdeen 2–1 in the 1978 Scottish Cup Final

Suited and booted – in May 1978 I was named the first-ever Players' Player of the Year, making it a double with my Football Writers' award

leg and they witnessed Rangers being taken apart. Cruyff was sublime. I had watched him on TV and studied that legendary trademark turn but, in the flesh, he was impossible to close down – he was just a player with unbelievable ability on the ball. But, midway through the first half, I thought I had him. Cruyff was hard up against the touchline and I made a fatal mistake. As I dived in for the ball, he did his trademark drag-back and I flew past him on to the track. What an embarrass-ment! But Cruyff did exactly the same thing to many, many players – even ones who were far better than me.

We were outclassed and went down 3–1 but it was a huge learning curve for me to play against quality footballers like Cruyff, Johnny Rep and Arie Haan and the others. The second leg in Holland saw more of the same although we did manage a better scoreline than we had at Ibrox. This time we went down 3–2 to lose the Super Cup 6–3 overall.

However, it had its positive side as the Rangers fans were beginning to respond to what they were seeing on the pitch. Genuine hope was in the air that we could go all the way in the championship and in the Scottish Cup.

We faced Hibs in the fourth round and more than 60,000 saw me score in a game that ended 1–1. In the replay at Easter Road, wee Tam McLean scored twice to send us into the next round and we took care of Airdrie and Ayr United to set up a show-down against Celtic in the final.

But the title was the Holy Grail. Every day Jock drummed into us what was expected and the team's form since that stut-tering start had been superb.

Pittodrie is never an easy venue for any Rangers team. As we fought out this duel with Celtic for their crown, a 2–2 draw against Aberdeen in the Granite City in the second last game of the season killed us off. We had lost just once in twenty-nine league games and missed out on the title by a single point.

Sure, it had been a major improvement on what had gone before and the fans appreciated we had given everything to try to win the title but again we had fallen short and that left Jock Wallace and the staff gutted.

We had one last chance to win something that season and that depended on the outcome of an Old Firm Scottish Cup Final – a tournament Rangers had not won since 1966.

I believe the teams that fought out that final were two of the finest of the decade. The build-up was intense. We were smarting from narrowly losing the league while Celtic had got themselves another championship flag. The citizens of Glasgow braced themselves for a real battle and, in front of an astonishing Hampden crowd of almost 123,000, the players did not let them down.

Celtic had a fantastic team at that time. The mix was spot on. The survivors from the great Lisbon Lions team – Billy McNeill, Bobby Murdoch and Jimmy Johnstone – blended with emerging talents such as Kenny Dalglish and Davie Hay. And it was Kenny who gave Celtic the lead midway through the first half before Derek Parlane drew us level in a pulsating tie. Seconds into the second half, we burst in front and Alfie Conn found the net. But Celtic hit back with George Connelly scoring from the spot.

It was to take one of the most famous goals in Scottish Cup Final history to settle the match. As he so often did, Tam McLean angled over a superb cross. I made a good connection with the header and, from the moment the ball left me, I felt it was in. In 1970, at the other end of the ground, I scored the goal that catapulted me in to what seemed like a fairytale and here it was happening again . . . or was it? Agonisingly, the ball came off the right-hand post and bobbled along Ally Hunter's goal-line for what seemed like an eternity. But then big Tam Forsyth appeared at the other post to somehow stab the ball over the line with his studs. As he wheeled away, I saw the look of sheer delight on the face of the man they called 'Jaws' and it will live with me forever. It couldn't have happened to a nicer guy. Tam had arrived that season from Motherwell and had become an instant hero.

It was no more than we deserved from the season. John Greig was in tears – *that* was how much it meant. We had a trophy for our efforts and every Rangers fan knew we had given them everything we had.

And so did the boss. In the dressing room, he praised us for our efforts and then he came and sat next to me. 'Well done, son,' he said, in a softer tone than I was used to. 'That meant a lot to the fans – we had to give them something today.'

I nodded in agreement.

'But this club has to be winning the title again,' he growled, the soft tone now gone. 'Cups are nice but it's no more than a good day out and a party.'

Jock was right. It was great to beat Celtic, at any time, but truly great teams have to be champions and that was a mountain we were still finding it difficult to climb. Celtic had a better team than us – that was fact. We were more than capable of beating them in one-off matches but it was a different story when it came to having the steel to become champions as they did season after season. And this was not to change in season 1973/74 as we suffered yet another massive disappointment.

We were a maturing side but we were not yet ready. In the league we lost to Celtic, Hearts and East Fife, dropping seven points in our first four home matches, and even at this early point, there seemed to be no way we could stop Celtic's charge to making it nine league titles in a row. Confirmation of this came five days into the New Year when Celtic beat us 1–0 at Parkhead. We were dead and buried. A month earlier, they had hammered us 3–1 at Hampden – with Harry Hood scoring a hat-trick – in the semi-final of the League Cup and another trophy was gone.

In Europe, it was the Germans who again masterminded our downfall. After beating the Turkish side Ankaragucu 6–0 over two legs in the first round of the Cup Winners' Cup, we travelled to Germany's westernmost state to play Borussia Mönchengladbach. There we crashed to a 3–0 defeat. After that, the second leg was always a long shot and, even though we played far better at home, we lost 3–2.

As if that was not bad enough, we then suffered one of our worst domestic results in years. Dundee came to Ibrox in the fourth round of the Scottish Cup and, in front of almost 65,000 fans, they thrashed us 3–0. It was the angriest I have ever seen Big Jock. He tore into the players, branding us a disgrace to the club.

That defeat ended any chance of a trophy for the season and, for only the second time since 1959, we even failed to qualify for any European competition.

Jock Wallace's trophy haul from his first two seasons was just one Scottish Cup. Celtic had racked up nine league titles in a row and were looking unconquerable. Rangers had not won the title since 1964. Kilmarnock won it in 1965 and, after that, Celtic had notched up nine in a row

I had a long conversation with the boss before we broke up for the summer. It was not often you saw him downcast. For the time being, he had the backing of the board but he knew the score. Two previous managers, Scot Symon and Davie White, had paid for a lack of success with their jobs. Jock knew one more season in the wilderness would see him suffer the same fate.

As 1974/75 approached, it was clearly last chance saloon for the manager and, most probably, many of his players. We had some good young players coming through and we still had a good blend with the old hands but, as early as the end of August, our hopes of success in the first tournament of the season were dashed.

St Johnstone, Hibs and Dundee should have been League Cup opposition that we could handle without too much difficulty and, indeed, Saints and Dundee were soundly beaten but, after losing 3–1 at Easter Road, we had to avenge that defeat in the final group game at Ibrox to progress. In the event, Hibs scored in the last minute to win 1–0 and we left the field to the familiar crescendo of boos from the 55,000-strong crowd. And it was no wonder the fans were raging – they thought this season was to be more of the same.

With the pressure mounting on the terraces and the dressing room, Big Jock set about getting a reaction from the players – and the response was to be magnificent.

After drawing our first league game at Ayr United, we went eleven games unbeaten, with ten wins and a draw. We beat Celtic 2–1 at Parkhead, the first victory there in six years, and the whole thing just took off. Every Saturday we ran on to the field expecting to win. Suddenly, we were genuine title challengers again.

With the two teams fiercely battling it out at the top, the Old Firm games would prove decisive. Having won at Parkhead, we had to do the same on our own turf when Celtic came across the city on 4 January 1975. It was the perfect time for Jock Wallace to pull off a masterstroke that left even his own players stunned.

Instead of playing skipper John Greig in the left back position, he switched us to 3–5–2, with Greigy moving into a defensive midfield berth. Inside six minutes, I had us in front from a Tam McLean cross. How many times had that combination worked for Rangers?

Greigy was all over Kenny Dalglish like a rash and the star Celt could not shake himself free. The tactics worked superbly and we ran out 3–0 winners.

Back in the dressing room, Jock had to pull some of us down from the ceiling. He knew the title had not been won that day but the victory certainly fired the players up. Beating Celtic twice in the league in one season! We had started to prove this was not a flash in the pan as had been the case so many times in the past.

But it was not all roses. In February, we were dumped out of the Scottish Cup by Aberdeen after a replay but it could have been a blessing in disguise. So much focus was on winning the league that nothing else mattered. We didn't even have Europe as a distraction. The two domestic cups? Well, we had won them a few times, anyway. The title was the one we wanted and we stormed through game after game.

And then the great day dawned. With five matches to go, one afternoon at Easter Road, we had the opportunity to win our first Scottish League Championship in eleven long, lean years.

The official attendance was given as just over 38,500 but it looked several thousand more than that. Three quarters of Easter

Road was filled with Rangers fans – they were on a title pilgrimage. When I went out to warm up, there was red, white and blue everywhere. In the dressing room, hardly a word was spoken. The atmosphere was tense, not least because our inspirational skipper Greigy was injured but Big Jock still listed him as a sub.

It was one of those days when words are unnecessary – a day when players look around them, look at one another, look at the manager and they realise there is no way they can't deliver.

Sure, we had games to spare if we needed them but we wanted it now – my God, we wanted it so much. To be part of the Rangers team that stopped ten titles in a row going to Celtic and be called a champion . . . Now that was a word not many in our dressing room had been associated with.

As is the case on such days of moment, things did not go entirely to plan. We lost an early goal to trail 1–0 at the break and, just to add to the tension, Sandy Jardine had missed a penalty. But, cometh the hour-mark, cometh the man. Colin Stein had only been back at the club for a few weeks, since we re-signed him from Coventry. Steiny had never lost the way to goal and he powered a header from a Bobby McKean cross past Jim McArthur and we were level. The Rangers end exploded – in fact, most of the stadium erupted.

We grabbed the game by the scruff of the neck and finished very strongly. With seconds to go, I was to witness one of the most emotional moments in my time in football. Greigy was shot, his season cruelly ended by injury, but Big Jock wanted his Captain Courageous on the pitch at the final whistle – he wanted Greigy to savour the feeling. So Jock sent Greigy on in place of Sandy Jardine and the two old pals, who had been through so much together in the name of Rangers, embraced on the touchline. Seconds later, the final whistle blew and we were there – Rangers were league champions!

My God, we had done it! I sank to my knees as delirious fans spilled on to the pitch. We'd spent eleven seasons without a title – and, for nine of them, we'd had to endure the sight of our greatest rivals hogging the game's major honour. I cannot begin to describe how good that felt.

In the dressing room, the champagne flowed and those long years of anguish disappeared like the bubbles. We had lost just two league games in the entire season. Rangers had been in the wilderness but Jock Wallace had dragged us back. And now, in the moment of his greatest triumph, he merely called for calm. 'Well done,' he said. 'Well fucking done. You have made Rangers the number one team in this country and I am so proud of every one of you. Go away and celebrate tonight and enjoy the last few weeks of the season. But this has to be the start for us. I never want to see Rangers waiting eleven years again for a title. You must have this feeling every year.'

It was a measure of the man. He was the manager of the team who had just become league champions but he felt it important to remind us the odd win every decade or so wasn't good enough. He wanted Rangers to dominate the way Celtic had – and he was about to get his wish.

The face of Scottish football changed as the 1975/76 season dawned. The old First Division was gone and had been replaced by the Premier Division. A new three-league set-up was designed to give the game a much-needed shake-up. It was a good decision at that time as there had been a lot of meaningless matches. Barring the odd intervention by Kilmarnock, Hearts and Dundee, the Old Firm had been fighting out the title for decades. That would not change but there was a feeling of excitement being generated by the restructuring. We had been the winners of the last-ever First Division and we definitely wanted to be the winners of the first-ever Premier Division.

Our League Cup section brought games against Motherwell, Airdrie and Clyde. We skated through, winning four and drawing two. That set us up perfectly for the first-ever Premier League game – the season opener against Celtic at Ibrox on 30 August 1975.

Celtic were seriously hurting after losing their iron grip on the crown and they too were determined to claim first blood. Old Firm games are never for the faint-hearted but this one was to have a real edge.

Kenny Dalglish, by this time showing why he was one of the very best in the game, gave the Parkhead men the lead three minutes before half-time. Eleven minutes into the second half, I got us back on level terms before Quinton Young sent the Rangers fans, in the near-70,000 crowd, wild when he struck the winner.

Wee Doddie MacDonald was sent off as the game got niggly but we hung on for a crucial win. It was not only two massive points on the opening day but also another huge psychological blow to our rivals. We were now the side with all the title ingredients going for us – strong at the back, solid in midfield, with the right balance of dig and guile, and plenty of power and pace up front.

We played some fantastic football and not even the disappointment of a second round European Cup exit to St Etienne could derail domestic domination that yielded an unbeaten run of twenty-one matches.

When we reached the 1975 League Cup Final, it was inevitably Celtic who stood in our way. There was little between the teams – but enough for Rangers. It took sixty-seven minutes before Alex MacDonald ended a trademark late run into the box with a stunning diving header to give us the trophy. One trophy in the bag by the end of October – it was early days but now there was only one side who could do the Treble. What an achievement that would be and Jock could taste it. He drummed it into us every day in training, as he bullied players to go that extra yard in games. I had never seen such hunger – we were relentless.

Defending our title had become an obsession and I fuelled it by scoring yet another Old Firm winner in the Ne'er Day encounter. When we swept past East Fife, Aberdeen, Queen of the South and Motherwell to make it to the Scottish Cup Final, the Treble was firmly in our sights.

When the great day of the opportunity to retain our title dawned, it was another away game – and this time it was in my hometown of Dundee. We got early to Tannadice where, like the year before at Easter Road, Rangers fans were everywhere.

'Let's keep it tight, lads, don't give anything away and a goal will come.' These were the words of wisdom from Jock Wallace as we headed on to the pitch.

The game kicked off with us keeping ball in our backline and then a long ball was launched into the United box. It came right into the danger zone – exactly the kind of ball I thrived on picking up. There was a United defender right up my arse but I used my strength to hold him off and roll him away. Then I turned and lashed the ball into the net. In the game that could see Rangers win the title, I had scored in twenty-two seconds. I held both arms aloft and looked to the main stand and there they were – the six Johnstone brothers. OK, they had been reared as United fans and maybe there were mixed feelings but they were all on their feet, cheering with all the other Rangers fans.

It was an unbelievable day for me and for the club. We had the League Cup and the Championship in the bag. One more hurdle, a Scottish Cup Final against Hearts, and we would have the clean sweep. What more emphatic way to send out the message that Rangers were well and truly back?

Throughout my career I loved playing alongside wee Tommy McLean. He was a fantastic talent with the heart of a lion and he was the architect of many of the goals that earned me high praise. I would never have enjoyed such a career if it hadn't been for his wonderful service. In the Hampden tunnel before the 1976 Scottish Cup Final, he held me back. 'Big man,' said the wee man, 'if we get a free kick in a decent position, this is the plan. Go to the back post and turn away from me. Then swivel quickly and make a front-post run. I'll find you. We'll only have one chance at it because they'll get wise to us after that.'

Tam McLean had a more accurate, more reliable delivery than Royal Mail. We used to say he could put the ball on a sixpence so finding my big noggin was never a problem.

The referee's watch must have been fast because the game, in front of a heaving crowd of 85,000, kicked off before the scheduled 3 p.m. start.

In the first minute, we got a free kick on the right. Wee Tam shoved Greigy out the way and bent over to place the ball. I glanced over to him and he nodded. I followed his instructions to the letter, drifting to the back stick before turning and racing across the box. Right on cue, the cross came in – perfection. I headed it into the net and Rangers had the lead after just forty-two seconds – and it *still* wasn't three o'clock. What a start to a cup final!

When Doddie fired home a daisy-cutter just before the break, we had one hand on the Scottish Cup – and the Treble.

To their credit, Hearts battled back in the second half but, with just nine minutes left, my second of the game sealed it before they got a consolation goal. The victory gave Rangers only the third Treble in the club's long and illustrious history. There can be no better achievement – winning the Treble proves, beyond all doubt, you are the best. It was a fantastic Rangers side and they were bossed by a guy who was emerging as one of the best managers in the history of the club.

Many observers put our success firmly down to the manager's motivation, his famous accent on 'character'. That was all they banged on about – 'character' – which was disrespectful to what Jock and his players had achieved. Jock Wallace was about so much more. He had a good grip on tactics and he got a unit together that played to its strengths. It was never going to be easy taking over from Willie Waddell but, in four seasons, we had won a Scottish Cup, broken Celtic's title dominance by winning the league and we had done the Treble.

Rangers were now the force the fans had been demanding . . . or were we? The following season can easily be summed up in one word – disaster. It was inconceivable that a Treble-winning team could end up with nothing but 1976/77 was a case of Rangers being so near, yet so far. I have been asked many times why, coming off the back of a Treble, things fell apart for us and I really don't know the answer. I believe we still had enough quality in the ranks to kick on from what we had achieved.

We were operating with maybe sixteen or seventeen players and the boss was asking the same men to put in hard shifts time after time. At the end of the 76/77 season, the likes of Sandy Jardine and Tam McLean had played in every game. So was it all just a bridge too far for some? Were some of the lads beginning to feel it in the legs after long, arduous seasons at the club?

We made a disastrous start in the league. With just eight points from eight matches, we'd drawn four of the first five. The defence of the Premier League title began at Parkhead and all looked well when I scored the opener nine minutes into the game but I was to rue missed chances as we drew 2–2.

After that, our form was patchy. We were cruising through the League Cup qualifying section with ease until we met Clydebank – we had to play them four times before we reached the semis. After the two legs had ended 4–4 on aggregate and we couldn't be separated, it took two play-offs before we finally won through.

Europe was another disaster – for the team and for me. Our opponents were the Swiss side FC Zurich. No one expected we'd have any problems beating them but they scored inside the first minute in the first leg at Ibrox. Although Derek Parlane equalised, they had shown enough to suggest the second game would be very difficult.

Considering they came from a country famous for its neutrality, you wouldn't think the Swiss would be out to start a war but that's certainly what it seemed like to me. I always played with shin pads on the back and the front of my legs, and how I needed them in Zurich. For the whole night, I was kicked non-stop, nipped from behind and even had the hairs under my arms pulled when opposition players 'helpfully' pulled me up after tackles. They had taken an early lead and were clearly prepared to do anything it took to defend it.

Unfortunately, it all got too much for me and I snapped. The Zurich player Zigerlig went through me one time too many so I got up and shoved him over. He performed the customary double somersault with pike and received a 9.9 from the referee. By the letter of the law, I had retaliated and I was sent off for the first time in my career. I felt I had let them team down but, given the provocation I'd been under, no one pointed any fingers.

We had all been poor in that match and we had crashed out of Europe, beaten by a team that Rangers should have swept aside with ease.

Worse was to follow. Aberdeen stood between us and a place in the final of the League Cup, a trophy we had won the season before. They crushed us 5–1 in that semi-final and it has to be one of the poorest performances I have seen from a Rangers team at Hampden.

The season hurtled along with no respite. It's hard to explain why but sometimes players just seem to watch as things go racing past them – terrible results come along and you do nothing about them. Although we were training hard and getting extra pelters from Big Jock, it seemed as if nothing could turn the season around. We never got out of first gear and, as Celtic bounced back from losing two titles in a row to reclaim the championship, we were left with a Hampden clash against the old foes to try to salvage some silverware and pride.

The 1977 Scottish Cup Final was decided by one of the most controversial penalty decisions ever – a decision that will go with me to my grave. With twenty minutes on the clock, Celtic's giant Icelandic player, Johannes 'Shuggie' Edvaldsson, powered on to a ball that hadn't been properly cleared from our box and directed it goalwards. I was on the goal line with both hands out from my body, ready to stop the shot. In those days, you weren't sent off for deliberate handball and I was prepared to take the chance that Celtic would miss what would be a certain spot kick rather than let Shuggie score. But the ball didn't go to either side of me as I had anticipated. It came straight at me and I quickly pulled my hands together in front of me to protect the family jewels.

I couldn't believe it when I saw the referee, Bob Valentine, pointing to the spot and saying I had handled the ball. There was no handball – it had hit me just above the privates. This was very sore, by the way, but not as painful as the decision. I was raging. I tried to argue the toss with Valentine but he waved me away in that dismissive manner he liked to use. My objections went unheard and Andy Lynch stepped up to score what turned out to be the only goal of the final.

I watched the highlights on TV that night. One of the pundits they had on to do the post-match analysis was ex-Celt Paddy Crerand and he was banging on about it being a stonewall penalty. I felt like putting my foot through the telly.

For God's sake, it was over twenty years ago so, if I did handle the ball, wouldn't it be a good time to confess now, in these warts-and-all pages? Not a chance – I swear I did *not* handle that ball.

Nowadays, when a ref makes a howler, you can watch a dozen replays from a dozen different angles and read eight pages of commentary in the papers but, back then, Mr Valentine's terrible decision, which cost us the chance of winning the Scottish Cup, was just accepted without question.

It brought down the curtain on yet another season it was best to forget. Jock gathered us around him before we headed off for the summer. He was hurting. Had all the progress been undone in one bad season? We were ordered to go away and clear our minds.

There would be personnel changes for the 1977/78 season. And they were to be key ones at that – Rangers were about to bounce back with a vengeance. During the summer break, Davie Cooper was signed from Clydebank and, a week or two into the new season, Gordon Smith arrived from Kilmarnock. They were two excellent Scottish players and getting them signed up was the best bits of business the club have ever done.

I had already liked the look of Cooper – he could really play – and Smith, an obvious goal threat, was to be my partner up front. Around the same time, Bobby Russell also entered the scene so here were three fine players who would add something different as we tried to get back to winning things. But there was to be no difference in our start to the season as we lost the first two matches – at Aberdeen and then at home to Hibs. The Rangers fans were already staying behind to chant their unhappiness with the management.

A win over St Johnstone in the League Cup, which had changed to a home-and-away format, bought us minor breathing space but our foray into Europe was to be another nightmare for me.

For the second season running, we drew Swiss opposition – this time, it was Young Boys of Berne. We beat them 1–0 at Ibrox and then had to try to survive another very physical battle in the second leg. I managed to grab us a goal before I was red-carded in Europe for the second successive season – if you can believe it. But I have to admit that I only had myself to blame. After getting clattered once too often, I retaliated –

again. The only bonus was the result. We drew 2–2 and so went through 3–2 on aggregate.

It's fair to say there was a fair amount of trepidation, both on and off the park, as we approached our next match – Celtic at Ibrox. The fans were bristling because of the start we had made and the new lads were still coming to terms with the pressure of life at a huge club like Rangers.

When Shuggie Edvaldsson put Celtic two up by the half-hour mark, the natives were distinctly restless but, this time, they needn't have worried. There had been the glimmer of a promise that this Rangers side could be something special and now that promise burst into startling reality. Digging deep, we pulled one back through Smith in the 53rd minute. We then went at Celtic big-time and I levelled the game twelve minutes later.

The game was heading for a 2–2 draw when up popped Smithy to grab a stunning winner. What a result! It was a major turning point and, after that, we hardly looked back.

There was disappointment in Europe when the Dutch side, Twente Enschede, knocked us out in the second round of the Cup Winners' Cup but, at home, after losing the first two games of the season, we were only defeated in one of the next twenty-three.

What's more, the team was a joy to watch – great football, great goals and I was on the score sheet in almost every game. My partnership with Gordon Smith was working a treat and the pin-point service we were getting from wee Tam on one wing and Coop on the other was creating chance after chance for us.

The highlight of our run to the League Cup Final was a 6–1 thrashing of an in-form Aberdeen side. That was one of the best domestic displays I had seen at that time, as we took them apart at Ibrox to march into another Old Firm final.

The final was an excellent match. Coop gave us the lead just before half-time after Gordon Smith had chased a lost cause to the byline and got the ball across. The trophy looked to be ours but, with five minutes left, Edvaldsson equalised so it was in to extra time. And Jock just went for it. He threw on the subs and Smithy bagged the winner with just three minutes left.

Just as had been the case two years before, we had bagged the first leg of the Treble. We stormed ahead in the title race and clinched the crown on the last day of the season when we beat Motherwell 2–0 at Ibrox. We finished two points clear of Aberdeen and a massive nineteen ahead of Celtic, who had seen their season collapse.

All that remained now was the chance at securing another Treble and it was duly delivered a week later when we beat Aberdeen 2–1 at Hampden in the Scottish Cup Final. I scored one of the most treasured goals of my career that day – a header past the Dons' Bobby Clark, a keeper who was notoriously difficult to beat. When the final whistle blew, it was one of the most satisfying moments of my life.

I think that second clean sweep in three seasons was the greater achievement of the two – the opposition was tougher and teams wanted to scalp us. We had been slagged off as a long-ball team with little skill but we proved everyone wrong and entertained along the way. I'm not saying that season was better than going all the way in Barcelona – they were different teams and different moments – but there was an unbelievable satisfaction about that second Treble, a feeling I had not expe-rienced since 1972.

Of course, the fact that, in goal-scoring terms, it was my

best-ever season didn't hurt. Almost everything I hit went in the net and I finished with thirty-nine goals. Gordon Smith, incidentally, scored twenty-six. I was named Players' Player of the Year and Scottish Football Writers' Player of the Year. I was immensely proud.

I was twenty-four and in the form of my life. I glanced across the dressing room at the man who had helped bring me to this moment. Big Jock was the first Rangers manager ever to win two Trebles – not a bad achievement for a man who had been written off by the press and deemed not good enough to be the manager of Glasgow Rangers. He was at the height of his powers and he had a talented squad that could be around for years. Now was the time to invest in the team, build on that foundation.

It was not to be. On 23 May 1978, just seventeen days after he had steered the club to another Treble, Jock Wallace resigned as manager of Rangers. I still shake my head today at the very thought of it.

10

SCOTLAND AND WORLD CUP WOE

Nothing can fill a footballer with more pride than representing your country and I look back very fondly on the fourteen caps I won for Scotland. But I will never forgive Ally MacLeod for the way he treated me during the 1978 World Cup Finals in Argentina. It had the effect of souring my international career and it capped a summer of hell for me as I came to terms with Jock Wallace's shock decision to quit Rangers. It also proved to be the beginning of the end of in terms of me pulling on the dark blue strip.

Back in 1973, playing internationally had begun so well for me when my journey with Scotland got underway down at the Racecourse Ground in Wrexham. On 12 May, the first Home International of that summer was to be played and, at the age of nineteen, I was chosen by Willie Ormond to start against Wales. I had a lot of respect for Willie – he was a good man and also a decent manager. He knew how to get the best out of people although, arguably, he had an advantage over other Scotland managers in that he was in charge of the best group of players any manager of a Scottish side has ever had. To see what I mean, you only have to look at the number of top players from that period who got very few caps.

In recent times, I've had to chuckle at some of the players

who have got a game for Scotland, especially under the hapless Berti Vogts. In the 70s and early 80s, they wouldn't have got a job carrying the hampers for the national side!

Willie Ormond told me I was getting the nod to start against Wales. I was to play in central defence, a role I had been filling for a couple of seasons at Rangers. There were around 18,000 people in the stadium and the atmosphere was great.

I've always felt sorry for the present-day players because they haven't had the chance to play in the Home Internationals. They were fantastic matches. From time to time, the idea of resurrecting them is mooted and, if it was up to me, I would have them back in a second. Every summer, you'd be up against the best players in Britain and, luckily enough, my Scotland debut was to be a winning one, with George Graham scoring twice as we beat Wales 2–0 on their own turf.

In midweek, we faced Northern Ireland at Hampden for my home debut. Unfortunately, we lost 2–1 and I wondered if Willie would drop me the following Saturday for the game against England at Wembley. To be honest, I half expected it as I was still fairly inexperienced at that level. But, the day before the game, I learned I was in the team for the Auld Enemy clash in front of just under 100,000.

I was still in my teens as I walked out on to a sun-bathed Wembley. The stadium looked as if it was decked end to end in tartan, with Scotland fans all over the place.

We started the game very well and put England under pressure although we fail to capitalise on it by taking the lead. I was up against Mick Channon, who was one of the best in the business at that time. He was far quicker than me and it was clear that he fancied his chances against this young kid. He didn't like it when I boxed clever, standing off him at just the right time to make up for the lack of pace should he get a run on me.

Overall, I was very pleased with my performance but we were hit with the ultimate kick in the you-know-whats when Martin Peters ghosted in, as he did so often in his career, to head England into the lead.

We then watched as Peter Shilton pulled off one of the best saves I've ever seen. He somehow twisted high to his left and, with the wrong hand, his right, deflected a goal-bound shot from Kenny Dalglish over the bar.

Beaten but unbowed, I had been thrilled with my first three caps in quick succession and I was to stay in Willie Ormond's plans for matches in Switzerland and at home to the mighty Brazil.

I'll never forget that match in late June against the Samba stars, nor the headlines that greeted me in the press the next day. 'JOHNSTONE SCORES . . .' reported the back page of the old *Evening Citizen*, 'FOR BRAZIL!'

As I'd done so many times in a Rangers jersey, I tried to play the ball back to my club keeper, Peter McCloy, after the brilliant Jairzinho had fired a cross into the box. Unfortunately, there had been no shout from Peter as he had come out from goal behind me to collect the ball and my pass-back bobbled into the net for an OG. To this day, Tom Boyd, who did likewise in the opening match of France '98, and I form an exclusive two-man club of Scotland players who have scored own goals against Brazil.

Those were the final internationals of 1973. The following season, Rangers made a decision that was to have a big impact on my Scotland career – when everyone was fit at Ibrox, I would be playing as a striker. There would be exceptions, of course – my versatility meant Jock Wallace could play me anywhere as needed – but, first and foremost, he wanted me as a striker. He was the boss and there would be no debate about it.

However, Willie Ormond had made it clear that he did not rate me as highly as other strikers he had at his disposal so there was to be no place for me in the 1974 World Cup Finals squad for West Germany. To be fair to Willie, I was still young and I didn't really expect to be a first pick and he did have the likes of Denis Law, Peter Lorimer, Kenny Dalglish and Joe Jordan to call on. I felt there would be plenty of chances for me but what a misconception that turned out to be.

Missing out on Germany still came as a blow as naturally I had ambitions of playing in my first World Cup Finals. Willie, in his defence, was very straight with players and he laid it on the line. He told me I would be selected in squads but there would be others he viewed as better for the striking roles. I had to admit it was decent management even if I didn't agree with him.

I don't think Jock Wallace was too amused with Willie's decision either but Rangers was always his main priority. Over the next three years, I played only five more times for Scotland, which is not a lot of games, really. I was no different from every other player – I wanted to play for Scotland – but there was a hell of a bunch of top players available at that time. I had to take it on the chin, as did many other very good players who, like me, will look back on their careers and maybe wonder if they should have had more caps.

Although I finished up with fourteen caps, I must have pulled out of fourteen squads. Big Jock would say to me, 'Listen, son, you are one of the most important players in this Rangers team.

I don't want you away there for three days training and then wasting your time getting on for ten minutes. We pay your wages. We decide what you do.'

So that's the way it was. If I was carrying a wee knock or the manager wanted me at home all week ahead of a crucial Old Firm game or an important Aberdeen match, I was told to pull out.

Given that Willie Ormond had already laid it on the line for me as far as my chances of getting a game was concerned, Jock felt I would be better off at Rangers. We were battling with Celtic for the league title right through the 70s and it was important not to have key players missing. And I would hazard a guess that the Celtic boys on the periphery of Ormond's plans were told to do exactly the same by Jock Stein.

The summer of 1976 saw me return to the Scotland fold and again it was for the Home Internationals. I played in the 3–0 home win over Northern Ireland and also the 2–1 win over England at Hampden.

After that, it was all change as Ally MacLeod succeeded Ormond in May 1977. I had not had much contact with Ally, other than as manager of Aberdeen when Rangers played them over a couple of seasons before he took the Scotland job, so I wondered what the story would be for me under him. I didn't have long to wait before I found out. Despite playing well for Rangers in the 76/77 season that had just ended, I was excluded from the Home Internationals. Was this a sign of things to come? It appeared the new Scotland manager didn't fancy me.

Scotland were attempting to qualify for the 1978 World Cup Finals in Argentina and Ally was under pressure to ensure the nation made it into a major tournament again. It was understandable that he would want to stand by the tried-and-trusted players who had been doing well in a qualification group that had included Czechoslovakia and Wales. MacLeod didn't want to rock the boat as we homed in on the finals.

However, I still hoped I'd get a chance and it came in February 1978 in a friendly against Bulgaria, a game we won 2–1. That was my introduction to life under Ally. I had heard stories about his unusual approach to things from other players. On his introduction to the Scotland squad, he had told them, 'Hi, I'm Ally MacLeod. I am a winner.' Such eccentric statements were to become something of a trademark – as was his bizarre behaviour.

His first problem was a lack of communication with the players. That had been one of Ormond's biggest strengths although, having said that, we used to take bets on how many seconds Willie's team talks would last. Normally, the winner would be between a minute and a minute and a half. Willie left it to players like Billy Bremner and Denis Law, the senior guys, to sort things out on the pitch. Ormond would say, 'You are the best eleven Scottish players I have. Play like you do for your clubs and that will do me.' And that was it. We would go on to the pitch and play. But Willie had our respect, something that, right from the off, MacLeod never appeared to have. I felt the job was too big for him.

In truth, the senior players ran his squads. For instance, if Scotland were playing away, MacLeod would say he wanted the squad to have a look around the stadium on the morning of the match, maybe suggest a light jog to get used to the pitch and the surroundings. But, if the players said they wanted to relax or go shopping instead, MacLeod would say, 'Fine.' Can you imagine the likes of Jock Wallace or Jock Stein allowing players to call the shots like that?

MacLeod found it difficult to see past the players who had been doing him a turn. He had Joe Jordan and Kenny Dalglish up front and my only chance of a game under him would be if any of the first-choice guys got injured. That was fair enough and there were a few players in the same position. But that didn't explain the serious personality clash between MacLeod and me. He would rarely speak to me one on one, like he did with other players. During training sessions, I felt he had no time for me and there was rarely any kind of dialogue. At team meetings, he would never mention my name and never catch my eye. Even when I did decent things on the training field, there was never a word of praise uttered. I have heard it claimed he disliked Rangers and that was why he didn't play me. Maybe there was something in that but one thing is certain – he didn't like me and I sure didn't like him!

By the summer of 1978, with Scotland's place at the World Cup Finals in Argentina secured, I was in the form of my life. I would say that, without a doubt, I had just had my finest season as a professional player. At the age of twenty-four, I had scored thirty-nine goals in a Rangers team that had just completed the domestic Treble. I was voted SPFA's Player of the Year and Scottish Football Writers' Player of the Year. Surely, with a World Cup around the corner, I would be in with a chance of playing?

There was a public clamour for my inclusion in the Scotland team. MacLeod didn't want me but how could he ignore a player who had just enjoyed such a successful season? In my heart, I always felt I would lose out but, in my head, I couldn't believe any manager would jeopardise his country's chances of progressing in a competition by excluding an in-form player just because of a clash of personalities. The very best managers in the business – the Steins, the Wallaces, the Fergusons – always put their teams first. I hoped MacLeod would see it that way but not one word of encouragement passed his lips and I believe the only reason I was included in the team for the Home Internationals was because he bowed to the pressure.

So, before our departure for Argentina in the summer of 1978, I had been in fine form and that was not to change when I took to the international stage. In the first game, which was against Northern Ireland at Hampden, I scored as we drew 1–1. Then, four days later against Wales, I produced arguably the best goal I've ever scored to really crank up the campaign to get me into the Scotland team for the finals. Archie Gemmill drove over a cross and I met it full on with my head from the edge of the box. It was a magnificent header and the ball thundered into the net to give me my second international goal in two matches and my forty-first of the season. Again we drew the game 1–1.

Come the weekend, when we faced England at Hampden, I was dropped in favour of Joe Jordan who had come back from injury. Little did I know then that my glorious header against the Welsh would be my last chance to score for Scotland under Ally MacLeod.

The whole country was going crazy before we left for Argentina and MacLeod was fanning the flames as he told the world Scotland feared no one. He loved the fact that England hadn't qualified and he got carried away. All that 'On the March with Ally's Army' stuff was total nonsense and it was ridiculous for any manager to become involved to that degree and build such expectations. It did nothing for him in the eyes of the players – not that many of them had much respect for him anyway as far as I could see.

I had always enjoyed a good relationship with the managers I'd played for, from the great Willie Waddell to Jock Wallace and even Willie Ormond. A manager's door should always be open, especially when it comes to dealing with players. People have asked me many times if I had clashed with MacLeod before the finals or why it was that he seemed to have a bee in his bonnet about me. There was no showdown. It was just crystal clear that we didn't like each other.

A few days before we left for South America, we were at our training base in Dunblane. I went to see him and I said, 'Before we leave, boss, I just want you to know I can do a job for you up front, in midfield or defence. I've played in all those positions for eight years now at Rangers and I think I can handle it. I just want to give you that option, should you need me.'

He looked straight through me. 'I'll be the judge of whether you can play in those positions. We'll see at the time – I might consider it.'

As he walked away, I could sense his rage. I think he felt I was too big for my boots because I was one of the bigger names at Rangers and because of the season I'd just had. But I wasn't trying to dictate to him or pick his team. I was simply trying to find some common ground between us – player to manager – and letting him know I was as keen as anyone else in the squad to play anywhere he wanted me to. Clearly, my approach hadn't gone down well and I think I sealed my World Cup fate there and then.

Now, every manager has a right to pick whoever he wants. He should never be influenced by players, fans, the media or anyone else. I did not expect to be chosen to play for Scotland simply because of the season I had just had with Rangers but what I did expect was some level of communication with the manager. If he didn't want me there, he shouldn't have picked me. Don't put a guy in the squad because the media and the public agitate to get him there. Ally MacLeod had no intention of playing me in Argentina. It would have taken Joe Jordan and Kenny Dalglish to show up on crutches before he would have considered giving me a Scotland jersey.

However, as we snaked down the A77 towards Prestwick Airport, leaving behind 25,000 fans who had turned up at Hampden to give us a victory parade before we had even kicked a ball, I still hoped and prayed that the man at the front of the bus would have a change of heart and give me a chance.

The Scotland squad that travelled to Argentina was:

Keepers – ALAN ROUGH, JIM BLYTH, BOBBY CLARK

Defenders – SANDY JARDINE, WILLIE DONNACHIE, MARTIN BUCHAN, GORDON MCQUEEN, STUART KENNEDY, TAM FORSYTH, KENNY BURNS

Midfield – BRUCE RIOCH, DON MASSON, ASA HARTFORD, WILLIE JOHNSTON, ARCHIE GEMMILL, GRAEME SOUNESS

Forwards – KENNY DALGLISH, JOE JORDAN, DEREK JOHNSTONE, LOU MACARI, JOHN ROBERTSON, JOE HARPER

Our problems started early as, in my opinion, those behind the planning took us to Argentina too early. The biggest danger you face when twenty-two players are away together is boredom. Nowadays, teams arrive at major tournaments maybe three or four days before their first game. In 1978, Scotland arrived in Argentina two weeks before our first game which was due to be played on 3 June against Peru. It was a major blunder.

The next problem was the base chosen. MacLeod and the then SFA secretary Ernie Walker had scouted out our HQ weeks before, and the manager had boasted to us in Glasgow they had selected an 'ideal' base from which to launch our bid for glory. But the hotel at Alta Gracia in Córdoba was a joke. With its massive perimeter fence, it was more like a prison camp than a hotel. The Scottish press quickly dubbed it 'Camp Doom' because of the state of the place. I don't think the swimming pool even had water in it! Not one player was happy with the standard of accommodation and it wasn't just griping for the sake of it. Clearly, MacLeod and Walker had different ideas of what was acceptable.

We got a friendly welcome in Alta Gracia from the locals who were lining the streets and waving wee Scotland flags. But we could see it was something of a one-horse town and, as we neared the hotel, the boys staring out the windows must have been thinking the same as me, 'What in hell are we going to do here for the next fortnight?'

We hadn't completed the check-in process before we had the first sign that MacLeod was not in control. An angry Martin Buchan had returned to reception appalled at the state of the room he had been allocated. Martin was accustomed to travelling first class with Manchester United and he would accept nothing less. 'My room is a joke,' he told the manager. 'I can't be expected to stay there.'

Without pausing for thought, MacLeod told Buchan he could have his room. It was amazing. Here was the manager accepting an inferior billet to keep one of his players happy. How did he know the rest of us were not about to demand a change of room? It was yet another pointer that the players, not MacLeod, were running this show.

News soon filtered through from the press about the luxurious hotels and bowling-green training pitches being enjoyed by the other finalists, which left us feeling even more like second-class citizens. Our training pitches were rutted and full of potholes and bore more of a resemblance to minefields. Joe Jordan and I suffered twisted ankles during the very first session. The players were scared to run full out for fear of picking up injuries that could rule them out of the biggest competition of their lives.

Back in the prison – sorry, hotel – we soon learned there was no need for a menu. In homage to the famous Monty Python 'Spam' sketch, the standing joke became, 'What do you want tonight? Steak, steak or steak?' We were offered nothing else. Patience was quickly wearing thin among a group of players who were used to being well looked after by some of the biggest clubs in the UK.

And it didn't help our mood that a major issue had yet to be resolved – the question of the bonuses we would earn in Argentina. Such matters should have been agreed long before we left Scotland so that the players would have clear heads for the most important thing – the football. But here we were days from the opening game and still it hadn't been sorted out.

There were sixteen players in the 1978 squad who all plied their trade in England. The home-based lads – like me, Sandy Jardine, Alan Rough and wee Joe Harper – were shocked by some of the figures the Anglos said they were earning in wages and bonuses. And the likes of Lou Macari, Gordon McQueen, Asa Hartford and Joe Jordan were unhappy at what the SFA were offering. Again, it highlighted the amateur nature of those in charge. They acted like they were running a church team instead of one of the sixteen best teams in the game about to start a World Cup. We did finally reach agreement before the opening match but little good it did us.

As far as the physical preparations were concerned, every-thing was fine – we worked just as hard on our fitness as any of the fifteen other nations. But in terms of getting ready to face the teams in our group . . . well, that was a different thing altogether.

Six months earlier, the draw had placed us in Group Four with Iran, Peru and Holland. MacLeod had labelled it 'the perfect draw' but there is no doubt that everyone involved with Scotland that summer totally underestimated the task in hand. It was taken for granted we would sail past Peru and Iran and that the Holland game would not matter as, with wins over Peru and Iran under our belts, Scotland would already have made it to the second stage by the time we came up against the Dutch.

But, as the first match in Córdoba drew nearer, we knew absolutely nothing about Peru. We had watched a few video-tapes and read things in the press but we received no break-down on them, nothing about the potential danger players or the style of football they played. Our manager had not deemed it necessary to watch them in person or even to send a trusted scout to look them over so there was no way he could help the team with any insights. To make matters worse, the Peru coaching staff had not been so criminally unprepared. It later emerged that they had an extensive dossier on us. They knew every detail about every Scotland player and, boy, did they put those details to devastating use.

Scotland's opening game of the 1978 World Cup remains one of the biggest disasters in the nation's footballing history.

After taking the lead through Joe Jordan, Scotland slumped to a shocking 3–1 defeat. The Peruvians equalised just before half-time and then added two more goals in the second half through the magnificent Cubillas who, at times, was toying with us.

The result hit the squad like a missile. We limped back to the hotel, painfully aware that the Scottish press would slaughter us for a totally inept performance and rightly so – it had been nothing short of shambolic.

MacLeod had promised World-Cup success and now he had to eat his words. But, to be fair to him, he endured the grilling from the media. He didn't dodge anything but he was beginning to fall apart.

With four days until our next match against Iran, the papers were full of all sorts of nonsense about what was going on in Alta Gracia. We would go for a coffee or a coke at the wee cafe down in the village and local snappers would sell on the pictures. We were accused of drinking and all sorts of antics but that was a complete fabrication by the press. I remember sitting on the patio area one afternoon with four or five of the guys and our entertainment consisted of throwing wee stones at the ants that were scurrying around. That was as exciting as it got in Alta Gracia. The boredom had us demented but that was about to change – and in the most sensational fashion.

After the defeat by Peru, Kenny Dalglish and Willie Johnston had been led away by FIFA officials to provide urine samples. It was standard procedure and there should have been nothing to worry about but, incredibly, wee Bud failed the test. Before the kick-off in Córdoba, he had taken two Reactivan pills, which are designed to increase mental alertness. These were used throughout British sport even though they were banned because they contained the substance Fencamfamin – something Willie was not aware of. Willie was a good friend of mine at Rangers – he still is. He was not the only player taking

Reactavin in Argentina. I believe there were three or four other guys who popped a pill to give them an extra kick but they have never admitted it. I won't name names – they know who they are – but wee Bud, being wee Bud, was the one who got caught.

He broke the rules and was done bang to rights but that did not excuse the way he was treated. You would have thought he had killed someone. Cop cars descended on our hotel in the dead of night. They threw a blanket over wee Bud's head and bundled him into a car. He was driven to the airport and Argentinean soldiers, guns waving, escorted him to a plane.

Bud's drug test failure became worldwide news and, as the press descended from ever corner of the globe, we tried to batten down the hatches.

The Scotland doctor, Dr Fitzsimmons, grilled every player on what medicines they might be taking – flu tablets, sleeping tablets, anything at all that, without them even knowing it, could get them into the same kind of bother as wee Bud was in. I piped up that I was using an inhaler to help me breathe, as training was hard in the tough, humid conditions. Despite my protests that I needed it, the inhaler was confiscated. The medical team were scared shitless someone else would fail a drug test.

The irony of the whole episode was that wee Bud was the kind of person who actually needed something to calm him down, not give him an extra surge! But that was lost on everyone, including the manager, who was now under siege from the media.

For all he appeared a flamboyant character in public, there were times when Ally MacLeod would withdraw completely from the players. When we were behind in matches, all he would tell us in the dressing room was, 'It will come, it will come.' After Peru, his stunned players needed more than that – they had to be lifted. But there was nothing coming from the top and we were about to stumble headlong into another disaster.

The game against Iran in Córdoba was the breaking point for me. Given the choice, I would have gone home there and then. Again I was a sub and again we took the lead after an Iranian own goal. Although we weren't playing well, it did look as though we could hold out for the win but Iran equalised on the hour mark and Scotland desperately needed another goal. When MacLeod turned to wee Joe Harper on the bench and told him to get stripped, I couldn't believe it. I've nothing against Joe – we were pals then and still are – but it didn't make sense to put him on. He had not been involved in the Home Internationals. And he hadn't even been by my side on the bench against Peru. As I was sitting there hoping for a start, he was in the TV gantry with Arthur Montford, broadcasting to the nation back home!

So, that was where I stood in Ally MacLeod's eyes. He preferred to put on a player – one of his former Aberdeen charges, remember – who hadn't even been deemed good enough to get stripped for the first match. I was raging but, when the game ended 1–1, my personal agony was swept aside in the tidal wave of chaos that engulfed the manager and the whole squad after that Iran result.

The team coach was parked beneath a flyover into the Córdoba stadium. Hordes of Scotland fans were there, with some hanging over the wall, and they were all giving us absolute pelters. You could not blame them. It had cost them fortunes to get to Argentina and we had rewarded them with possibly the two worst results in the nation's history. I stared at the ground, wishing it would open and transport me home right then. And it looked like that was where we were all headed now – out of a tournament some people had us believing we could win. Back home, the media were having a right go at us but, again, MacLeod did not duck the flak.

Defeated by Peru and managing only a draw against Iran, we had to beat the classy Dutch by three clear goals to stay alive. I knew there was no way I would kick a ball against Holland. The press were asking what I had done – why the manager wasn't picking me – but there were no answers and, by this time, MacLeod was falling apart.

Before the Holland game, he took his usual seat in front of the massed media and a stray dog wandered past to his left. MacLeod looked at it, held his hand out, sighed and said, 'I think you are my only pal in the world.'

Behind closed doors, the stress he was under had become even more evident. One of the players went to his room one morning before the Holland match and found MacLeod curled up in a ball on a couch in the lounge area adjoining the bedroom. 'What are you doing, boss?' he asked. 'Are you OK?'

'I'm fine – there is a spider in the bedroom.'

'Well, why don't you just kill it?'

'Oh, no – remember Robert the Bruce and the spider? I can't do that – it might be bad luck before the Holland game.'

And, in typical Robert-the-Bruce fashion, Scotland were to upset all the odds against a mighty foe.

In what was probably the only sensible move MacLeod was to make in the three games, Graeme Souness came in to the starting line-up. It had been a monumental error not to play Graeme. He had just finished a superb season at Liverpool and should have been in the middle of the park, calling all the shots. The difference having him in the team made was glaring.

This time the game was played in Mendoza and Rob Rensenbrink scored from the penalty spot to put the Dutch ahead but, before half-time, Kenny Dalglish had equalised against a side that was fancied to go all the way. After that, it became the Archie Gemmill show. Just moments into the second period, he knocked home a penalty to put us ahead and then he scored the goal which was later voted Scotland's Greatest Ever to make it 3–1.

As I sat on the bench, not believing what I was seeing, I thought, 'Christ, we are going to pull this off!'

But Jonny Rep scored a peach to make it 3–2 and we were out.

I didn't exactly jump up and celebrate Rep's winner but I can't deny that, deep down, there *was* a part of me that was relieved. I had endured a nightmare under MacLeod and I didn't want to be there for another week. Two days after the Holland game, we were on our way back to Scotland and I have to say that I've never packed a suitcase so quickly as I did for the flight to Prestwick. I think a lot of the squad felt the same way. We all wanted to go home and at least the Holland game had given the punters something to celebrate.

It later emerged that, because of wee Bud's failed drug test, we could have been tossed out of the competition by FIFA anyway – no matter what the result against Holland had been.

Looking back, I feel only four of our players emerged from Argentina with any credit. Archie Gemmill was a fantastic Scotland player and did not deserve any stick. I also felt Asa Hartford had done well and was a good teammate when others were hiding. Martin Buchan never gave up, even when we were all over the place, so I don't think any fingers of blame could be pointed at him. And then there was Graeme Souness. He was only used once but everyone could see he was one of the best footballers in the world.

Apart from them, the squad let the country down. There were many inquests and the press claimed we had been too busy boozing and partying to care but that's absolute rubbish. The fact that we were badly prepared was the fault of the manager but the players must shoulder a large portion of the responsibility. That squad should have been good enough to make it into the second round from a group that contained Peru and Iran.

On the flight home, I walked to the front of the plane to see Ally MacLeod and by this time he was a broken man. He knew we would be engulfed by a media scrum at Prestwick, with the press desperate for players to spill the beans about all the rumours. Normally I would have left a manager alone in his own world but I had something important to tell him. 'I just want you to know I am extremely disappointed you didn't see fit to use me once over there,' I said.

'It was my call and I'll live and die by that,' he told me.

'That was your decision but I don't want to be considered again for Scotland while you are the manager.' And, with that, I turned and walked back to my seat.

I could not give the man any commitment after that. I didn't know what the future would be for him – and, as it turned out, it was a few months before he did get the sack – but I went public and told the press I no longer wanted to play for Scotland if Ally MacLeod was manager.

It wasn't me being a bighead – it was simply that I could not go on playing under a man who had treated me the way he had. He knew we needed a goal but he'd refused to call on the services of a player who had just scored forty-one that season.

The Argentina experience wrecked my Scotland dreams. I wasn't heading home thinking, 'Oh, well, there's another World Cup in four years so maybe I can play at that.' I spent the whole flight home mulling it over and I decided that my club was to be my top priority.

When Scotland squads were named in the future, I didn't even bother to look at them. By the end of the Argentinean World Cup, I had thirteen caps and I was happy to accept there would be no more. People might find that strange as I was only twenty-four and should have had many years of international competition ahead of me but I had been left with a bad taste in my mouth and I had no time for the SFA set-up.

As it happened, I did play one more time for Scotland one more time. It was on 19 December 1979 in a 3–1 Hampden defeat to Belgium in a European Championship qualifier and Jock Stein was the manager.

I have no regrets. Sure, I could have had maybe double the caps I've got but I treasure the fourteen I did receive.

As for Argentina, I'm glad finally to get it off my chest after almost thirty years. The way I was treated is something I will never forget.

11

A RELUCTANT CAPTAIN

Willie Waddell peered straight through me over the top of the specs he always had perched halfway down his nose. The new season was approaching fast and he wanted my name on a new contract. The Deedle was not interested in my Argentina anguish. Neither would he be sympathetic if he knew the uncertainty I was suffering as I sat in his office. As far as he was concerned, I owed Rangers as much as they owed me. It was decision time.

I had finished 1977/78 on the ultimate high after my finest season in football – forty-one goals and the double Player of the Year awards. At twenty-four, I was on fire. But, since then, I had also taken two major hits. Jock Wallace had sensation-ally resigned as manager of Rangers, leaving me deeply upset with the club's attitude towards a man I was so close to. And I had suffered badly at the hands of Ally MacLeod at the World Cup Finals. I was restless. The long hours spent in South America had given me plenty of time to mull over my future. I'd had eight seasons at Rangers, a European Cup Winners' Cup success, two Trebles in the space of three years and I was thinking it was maybe time to move on.

I had informed the club of my feelings but they were about to tug at my heartstrings. They appointed John Greig as successor to big Jock and I think they felt it would sway me.

I roomed with Greigy on trips and we were good mates. I respected him so much. He was a true Ranger in every sense of the word. Jock Wallace and John Greig had been the biggest influences on my career. With him as manager, how could I leave? I had been distraught at Jock's news. He had just guided Rangers to their second Treble in three years, for God's sake! What could go so terribly wrong?

I'll tell you what. Hours after his shock announcement, Jock told me he was the *fourth* highest-paid manager in the league. I think he asked for more money, they said no and so he chucked it – simple as that. I see no other explanation because Jock was Rangers through and through. The last thing I said to Jock was not to take the vacant manager's job at Leicester City – I felt it would be a major step down from Rangers – but, of course, he did take it.

Greigy was on the golf course when he got the call from Willie Waddell to come to Ibrox for talks. Within twenty-four hours, he was the new Rangers manager – straight from the dressing room to the dugout.

And where did that leave me? I had been thinking that a change of manager could be the perfect time for me to move south. During my long chats with the Anglo boys in Argentina, I'd heard about their lifestyles and the big wages they were earning and maybe it had all turned my head.

The guys at Rangers and Celtic could easily have plied their trade in England and been successful but there was this invisible tie to their clubs. Loyalty was far more evident than it is now. To put this in perspective, Scotland keeper Alan Rough had a part-time job while playing with Partick Thistle. For me he was up there with Peter Shilton, his England counterpart, but Shilts didn't have to take on two jobs!

I had been approached, through third parties, and asked if I was interested in signing for Spurs and Arsenal. The money on offer was more than double the £240 a week I was on at Rangers and, like any normal young guy, I was tempted. I could play in England with all the big names and it would be a chance for me, at twenty-four, to move my game up a level. It was also a crucial time in my personal life as I was getting married that summer and it was the kind of move that would set us up for the next few years. I had met my fiancée Marion through mutual friends and I was looking forward to settling down.

Being brutally honest, the standard of football in Scotland was not impressing me. Sure, the Old Firm matches were excellent and we still had Europe every year but the rest was becoming a bit boring.

The papers were full of speculation that I would go because of Jock's departure. But then the club appointed Greigy. We had not been able to talk much since he was put in charge and I wondered if it would change things between us. Could I still joke with him? Could I still call him Big Ears? Greigy was no longer one of the boys. He would be boss. Was he ready for that? He was a great player and a fantastic leader on the pitch and in the dressing room but would it be possible for him to make the leap from player to manager without any experience? And, if I pledged myself to be by his side, how easy would it be for me to get out if things started to go downhill? My head was all over the place.

'Sandy and Bomber have signed – do you want to be the odd one out, Derek?' Willie Waddell challenged me across his desk. A look of disdain came over his face. 'And what about John? Are you honestly considering not signing this contract?

Are you really? You don't want to play for him? Replace him as captain?'

My eyes flashed up from the floor. 'Captain? Fuck,' I said to myself. Another heartstring had been tugged. I was now being offered the captaincy of Rangers as part of this new deal.

Willie Waddell, wonderful winger that he had been, could also talk a good game. But, at that moment, Sandy Jardine and Bomber Jackson had not signed their deals – the crafty Deedle was trying to reel us in one at a time, using the same bait.

I told him I had been offered deals with major clubs in England but he carried on as if he had never have heard me. 'You came to us at sixteen and this club has been good to you, Derek.' As far as he was concerned, nothing I had given in return could match that. This was Rangers and the good of the club came before everyone. 'Now, I understand what you're saying about the finances, Derek, but, if we can maybe look at this new contract . . .'

Two minutes later, I had signed on again at Rangers. I didn't want to be captain and I told Willie I would rather just be a player under Greigy. I never saw myself as captain material and Rangers captain? What a position of importance that is. I liked a few beers and enjoyed going out on the town but you have to act in a certain way when you are captain of Rangers. It wasn't for me and I tried to tell Willie that signing a new deal would be enough and just to let it go but he insisted.

The press were informed I had signed a new contract, I was happy with the terms and I was the new Rangers captain. I had signed for an extra £10 a week, taking my wages to £250 – half of what I had dreamed of earning in London.

Greigy adapted well to his new position. He commanded total respect from men who, just a few months previously, had been his teammates. On the training ground he was good. Despite never having been on coaching courses or taken any badges, he had a great knowledge of the tactics and formations that he felt we should deploy but, just like every other manager, the real test of his ability would come with the results.

Our defence of the title got off to a very poor start. On the opening day, St Mirren made the short journey from Paisley and a late winner from Bobby Torrance spoiled John's first competitive match in charge. We lost the first Old Firm game of the season 3–1 at Parkhead and, four days later, we travelled to face the mighty Juventus in the European Cup first round first leg. This was no ordinary Juve side. They had nine members of the Italian World Cup squad in their ranks. The Scottish press had their headlines ready – 'Torrid In Turin'.

It was Greigy's first foray into Europe as manager and, given the standard of opposition, he opted to try to keep things tight. Sandy Jardine played a sweeper role, Alex Miller and Kenny Watson came in and wee Tam McLean was dropped. Inside eight minutes, we had lost a goal when Virdis scored but, after a real backs-to-the-wall display, we managed to escape with just a one-goal defeat.

There was a real feeling we could see them off in Glasgow and, two weeks later, I played my part in one of the finest results Rangers have ever achieved in Europe. Everything clicked for us that night. The Italians were one of the fastest sides I'd seen but we ran rings round them and reduced them to nothing. A goal in each half, from Alex MacDonald and Gordon Smith, saw us through 2–1 on aggregate. We were awesome.

In the second round we drew the Dutch cracks PSV Eindhoven. They were a major side at that time and had never lost a European match at home so we knew that taking a lead from Ibrox would be crucial if we wanted to make the quarter-finals. We had our chances but PSV were dogged and it was stalemate at Ibrox. With their impressive home record, the second leg was considered a formality.

Greigy worked so hard on the tactics. We felt a scoring draw would be our best chance of getting through and his last words to us were, 'Keep it tight.' PSV scored inside a minute. Tam Forsyth mistimed his header and Harry Lubse lashed the ball past big Peter McCloy.

Our performance after that was one of the bravest I've seen from a Rangers team. We took the game to the Dutchmen, who had stars such as the twins Willy and René van der Kerkhof in their ranks. At half-time we were still a goal down but Greigy got in about us and the message was clear. We were still alive and, when Alex MacDonald converted a Tam McLean cross, we were level.

I think that goal stunned us as much as it did the PSV fans. We were still celebrating when PSV raced up the pitch and made it 2–1, with Deijkers putting them back in front. Step forward Big DJ. With twenty-four minutes to go, Tam fed Kenny Watson and he smashed a cross into the box. I got a flick on it and the pace on the ball saw it fly into the net to make it 2–2. If that score line remained, we'd go through on the away goals rule but we never sat back and we sealed a magnificent victory with one of the best goals I've seen a Scottish side score away from home in Europe. Tam McLean had been immense all night and it was fitting he was involved. He slipped a brilliant pass to Bobby Russell, who had made a superb run from midfield, and he showed all the composure in the world to slot the ball past van Engelen. We had done the impossible. PSV had been scalped at home for the first time and we were now being talked about as possible European Cup winners.

That game in Eindhoven galvanised us under Greigy. We started to believe the season could indeed bring us silverware. The European Cup? Why not? We had beaten the champions of Italy and Holland and had drawn Cologne in the last eight but that was not until March.

It was time to focus on domestic matters and the team raised its performance levels in the knowledge that the home fires had to be stoked. By Christmas, we were fourth in what was a very tight league. Just three points separated the top half dozen, with Dundee United ahead on twenty-three points. We had reached the final of the League Cup – again – after beating Celtic in a dramatic semi-final at Hampden just a couple of weeks before Christmas. Alex Miller and Tommy Burns were sent off as Jim Casey scored an OG in extra time to take us through 3–2. Aberdeen would be our opponents in March.

So everything was going well under John Greig. Off the back of a Treble and the shock exit of Jock Wallace, we had managed to put ourselves in line for a wonderful season. We had the players and we had the belief so now it was time to deliver – to start writing the history of a new Rangers era.

Sickeningly, the first chapter would not include me as an ankle injury ruled me out of the first leg of the quarter-final in Cologne. Greigy told me not to take any risks, even though I would probably have limped on to the field. He wanted me fit for the second leg and the other massive games we had coming up.

In Germany, Peter McCloy pulled off a string of superb saves to keep us in the tie but we were finally breached in the 57th minute when Dieter Muller scored with a far-post header. It wasn't the worst result but Cologne were strong and the return at Ibrox was going to be very tough.

I started on the bench. The plan was to throw me on if we couldn't get a goal. Billy Urquhart had come into the side and it wasn't to be his night. We fell behind just two minutes into the second half and again Muller was the executioner. Now we needed three goals to stay in the tournament. Big Billy missed a couple of snips and, even though Tam McLean scored late on, it was all over for us.

We were devastated in the dressing room. I honestly believed the team was good enough win the European Cup that season but we had fallen short.

The defence of the Treble wouldn't be a bad consolation, though, and it was still very much on.

First up was the League Cup Final against Aberdeen and we played them off the pitch. They didn't like it, and it turned into a stormy match. The Dons took the lead on the hour mark and then I was involved in an off-the-ball incident with big Doug Rougvie. He booted me off the ball and was rightly sent off despite protests from Aberdeen players and their bench that I had dived.

Alex MacDonald scored the equaliser and then Bomber Jackson grabbed the winner in the last minute. It was my first trophy as captain. What a moment it was, holding up that cup in front of a delirious Rangers support. 'I'll have a bit more of this,' I thought to myself.

With that first leg of the Treble in the bag, the momentum just grew and grew. We wanted it so badly and, after a replay in which I scored late on against Partick Thistle in the Scottish Cup semi-final, it was edging ever closer. Hibs would be our opponents in the final.

A crucial league clash with Celtic loomed in early May. Indeed, we had to face our old rivals twice in the space of three weeks. Davie Cooper was on a different planet in the first Old Firm match, which had to be played at Hampden as Ibrox was being rebuilt. He tore Danny McGrain apart and when Alex MacDonald popped up, as he so often did, with a second-half winner, we had victory and a one-point lead at the top with four games to go.

The Scottish Cup Final against Hibs turned out to be an epic – in length if nothing else. On 12 May, the teams scrapped out an untidy 0–0 draw at Hampden and, four days later, the replay again ended with the scoreline deadlocked, forcing a third match.

Before then, though, we had a crucial trip to Parkhead to deal with – a game that would more or less be a title decider with us one point ahead and three matches to go.

Bobby Russell gave us the perfect start with a goal after just nine minutes and, when Johnny Doyle was sent off ten minutes into the second half, the game looked to be swinging our way. But Roy Aitken had other ideas and he dragged Celtic up by the bootlaces. He made it 1–1 before George McCluskey had the Hoops 2–1 ahead. Inside two minutes it was 2–2, Doddie MacDonald again scoring in an Old Firm game. The draw suited us better than Celtic but nothing prepared us for the finale. Bomber Jackson scored an OG with five minutes to go. It was a disaster and, when Murdo MacLeod rasped in a scorcher to make it 4–2, we sank to our knees.

That was the sickest I have ever felt after a football game. I knew we had lost the title, even though there were two games to go. It was a crushing blow for the team and obviously for Greigy, who had seen a League Championship in his first season wrestled away in such dramatic circumstances.

A week later, we had to lift ourselves for the second Scottish Cup Final replay against Hibs and, at long last, we had a result. I scored twice before Arthur Duncan conceded an unfortunate OG in extra time to give us a 3–2 win. Greigy's first season had ended with two cups and a journey to the last eight of the European Cup but the league title disaster at Parkhead had shattered us. Such was the manner in which we had lost to Celtic that it was hard to get it out of our heads.

Strangely, I felt re-invigorated to a degree. If we could rebuild over the summer and get off to a good start, then maybe it had been the right decision to stay at the club under Greigy. Little did I to know Rangers had one foot on a slippery slope to unbelievable mediocrity.

I had won the title in 1978, my third league winner's medal. Never did I believe it would be my last, but a pattern was beginning to emerge at the club. There were bad signings and some injuries – in fact, not much was going right. I traced it all back to that last-gasp defeat to Celtic at the end of the 1978/79 season. If we had won the title that year, I think it would have acted as a springboard. Instead, off the back of that devastation, Rangers spiralled into freefall.

We began the 1979/80 season in decent enough spirits. Greigy freshened the squad up a bit but there was a lack of quality coming in that did concern me plus the directors did not appear to be moving with the times. Here was the biggest club in Scotland but there was still a bit of stubbornness about the whole thing. It was as if Rangers, because of what we had achieved in the past, had a right to success. While the other teams moved forward, we seemed to sit back and wait for it to happen. It turned out to be a wretched campaign and we won nothing.

The home form was fine but, away from Ibrox, we were dreadful and we lost fourteen out of thirty-six league matches. We were not even good enough to qualify for a place in Europe. It was a disgraceful season and the pressure mounted on Greigy and the players. By the end of October, we were faltering in the championship, Aberdeen had thrashed us 5–1 on aggregate in the League Cup, a tournament we had dominated in recent years, and, in the Cup Winners' Cup, we'd gone out to Valencia.

We had travelled to Spain for the first leg and produced another marvellous display of disciplined football. The brilliant Argentine, Mario Kempes, had fired Valencia ahead midway through the first half with a free kick but wee Tam McLean popped up to square things just before the break, giving us a crucial away goal. Peter McCloy was superb. He made a string of great stops and even saved a penalty from Rainer Bonhof with just ten minutes to go.

Ibrox was set up for another massive European night but, when Sandy Jardine scored an OG just fifteen minutes in, our place in the quarter-finals of the Cup Winners' Cup was disappearing over the horizon. I managed to get us back into the game but Kempes was brilliant that night. He scored two excellent goals to bury us 3–1. For the fans, it was yet more disappointment in a Rangers side that had badly let them down. It was becoming a familiar story.

The Scottish Cup emerged as our only chance of salvaging something from the season. I had found the net against Dundee United and Hearts and again against Aberdeen with a late semi-final winner to set up a showdown with Celtic, who had just lost the league title to Aberdeen by a point. It turned out to a game to be remembered . . . for all the *wrong* reasons.

A RELUCTANT CAPTAIN

Let me say right away that the 1980 Scottish Cup Final was not the best of matches but I take full responsibility for Rangers not winning the trophy. I had chances in the game that I would normally have stuck away. As a striker, I would ask my teammates to set up the goalscoring opportunities and I would do the rest. Usually, you could bank on me scoring about once in every three chances but not that day. In the games leading up to the final, I had been badly off form and I let the team down.

The game went to extra time and it seemed to be drifting towards a replay, with players from both teams looking very tired. But then Danny McGrain tried a speculative shot from outside the box and, as the ball fizzed into the area, George McCluskey stuck out a foot and diverted it into the opposite corner of the net. What a fluke! The Celtic hordes went wild and, when the final whistle blew, I just wanted to get off the field. I hated losing – especially to Celtic – and what made matters worse was the fact that I had been to blame.

As we sat in the dressing room in silence, our spirits crushed, news filtered through there had been a pitch invasion and fans were fighting running battles. We didn't know the scale of the riot – if something like that happens while players are still in the dressing room, they seldom do know – but, when I saw the pictures later, I was horrified. The scenes that went around the world from Hampden that day shamed the Scottish game. Fans stormed at one another from the opposite ends of the ground and mounted police charged both ends, trying to restore order. A good friend of mine, the photographer Eric Craig, was struck on the head by a bottle and sustained a serious injury and, at the end of the day, there were scores of injuries and 210 people were arrested.

Given the frustrating season they had witnessed, the defeat to their old rivals was maybe too much for many Rangers fans but that was no excuse for one of the blackest days in the history of football in this country.

It turned out to be a watershed in our game. An alcohol ban was imposed at football grounds and the post-match pictures of the huge mountain of beer cans and bottles that had been cleared off the vast Hampden terraces became a thing of the past. Except for a handful of isolated unsavoury incidents after that notorious 1980 riot, the Old Firm fans have never behaved so badly and thank God for that.

The final brought the curtain down on what had been probably my worst season since joining Rangers. With no European football, domestic matters were all we had to deal with as the 1980/81 season began.

Greigy tried to change the pre-season work to get the squad fitter but there was still no real investment in the team. Given that we had just had a barren campaign and had now gone two years without a title, it came as a major surprise that no one upstairs was beginning to sound alarm bells.

Nevertheless, we started the league season in amazing form – undefeated in the first fifteen matches and at last threatening to challenge for the title. A superb 2–1 win at Parkhead, courtesy of a last-minute winner from Alex Miller, an 8–1 thrashing of Kilmarnock at Rugby Park and a 3–0 home win over Celtic were the highlights.

By the start of November, we were bang in contention and feeling confident about what lay ahead. OK, the League Cup had gone, with Aberdeen again knocking us out over two legs, but we had won that trophy often enough. The league was the real deal and John Greig finally had the team looking like contenders. And that makes it all the more difficult to explain why the wheels came hurtling off the Ibrox wagon.

A string of draws against the likes of Partick Thistle and Airdrie, teams we should have been murdering, started the rot. That led to problems in the dressing room and we had too few players in the team with the kind of character that you need to stop the slide.

When Celtic beat us 3–1 at Parkhead in February, we collapsed. We'd gone from a position of strength in the autumn to finishing a miserable twelve points behind our bitter rivals. You couldn't blame the fans for going potty. Season after season, Rangers had made an art of systematically falling apart. Cups were the only thing we seemed capable of winning and – just like the season before – the only thing left to win that season was the Scottish Cup. This time, however, against Dundee United, we were to be successful.

I reported for training as normal on the Monday before the final. I had been out the night before with wee John MacDonald and Davie Cooper and, to be honest, I was feeling a bit worse for wear. In training, I could not kick my own backside. Greigy smelt the stale booze and wasn't happy. After training he asked what the hell was going on. When I told him, I didn't see the next move coming. Greigy said I would not be considered for the Scottish Cup Final against Dundee United on the Saturday and that I had overstepped the mark by going out drinking. I fired back that it had been a weekend, a full six days before the match, but he was having none of it.

After the two poor seasons we had just endured, John was under serious pressure and now he felt his captain was letting him down. I was out and wee John and Coop were dumped on the bench. I remember sitting in the stand at Hampden and wondering if I had played my last game for Rangers. I had fallen out with Greigy and, as far as I could make out, the club was a shambles and no one knew what direction we would stagger in next.

I have to be honest and say that part of me wanted the final to go to a replay so that I'd have the chance of one last game if this was to be the end for Derek Johnstone at Rangers. In the last minute, with the match tied at 0–0, Rangers were awarded a penalty. Ian Redford stepped up to take it but Hamish McAlpine made the save and we had the replay I craved.

On the Monday morning, Greigy called me over. 'You are starting the replay,' he said.

'OK, boss, that's great,' I replied.

I didn't want to have it out with John but I felt he had cut off his nose to spite his face. Now I was determined to win the cup for the fans. John and Coop were also reinstated and the impact was immediate. We destroyed Dundee United 4–1, with Coop producing a memorable display and wee John scoring twice, and, at last, we had won a trophy after two years of pain. But was that good enough for Rangers? Were we now nothing more than a cup team?

As captain of Rangers, I felt it more than most. Not many of the old guard were still around from the days when winning trophies was all we knew. Now we were a joke. The fans were dwindling away, disillusioned that the so-called New Firm, Aberdeen and Dundee United – never mind Celtic – were well ahead of us. We were no more than also-rans.

Every summer in the dressing room, we had heard rumours that there would be a change at the top – that the club would be sold and investment brought in – but the 1981/82 season was fast approaching and it was more of the same. There had been no decent signings and no money was being spent.

A young striker called Ally McCoist had been making a real name for himself at St Johnstone. It was widely known he was a Rangers fan and the club made a move to sign him. We bid £300,000 but Sunderland bid £400,000. The Rangers board would not push the boat out and so McCoist went to the north-east of England club in August 1981. That summed it up for me. If that was the level of Rangers' ambition and with that kind of leadership, there was never going to be a sustainable challenge.

Sure, we would have our moments – the odd runs of winning games and periods when we would flirt with being a force – but the squad was simply not good enough and I was part of that. I could see it, so could the fans and so could the outside world but those who mattered just seemed to believe that some kind of magic wand would fix it – this was Rangers, after all.

As before, the season promised something but, unable to mount a sustained challenge to Celtic, we again finished third in the league. By Christmas, we were seven points behind them in the league and we'd gone out of the Cup Winners' Cup in the first round after losing 4–2 on aggregate to Dukla Prague. Our old favourite, the League Cup, had provided the shaft of light. Despite being behind to Dundee United in the final in October, the team staged a remarkable comeback to win 2–1. Davie Cooper and Ian Redford scored inside the last fifteen minutes to flatten Tayside dreams again.

I was beginning to struggle with ankle and knee problems. It had been non-stop football for me since 1970 and now, twelve years on, injuries were beginning to take their toll. I had the heartbreaking blow of being ruled out of the 1982 Scottish Cup Final against Aberdeen with that on-going knee injury. As it happened, the game was maybe not such a bad one to miss. The Dons recovered from the loss of an early John MacDonald goal to batter us 4–1 – another disaster.

By this time, it had been four years since Rangers had last won the championship. While the club's record signing fee had been broken by buying Craig Paterson from Hibs for £225,000, I believed that not enough had been done over the summer to suggest that season 1982/83 would be any different from what had gone before. Sadly, I was correct.

We drew five of the first seven league games and showed all the old frailties. No one any longer viewed us as title material and apathy had replaced anger among the support.

As always, we made a good fist of it in the cup competitions. We also had a fine 2–0 aggregate win over Borussia Dortmund in the first round of the UEFA Cup but we couldn't repeat the feat against another team of Germans in the second round. I scored at Ibrox as we beat Cologne 2–1 in the first leg but, in the return match, we were blown away. Cologne scored four times in the opening twenty minutes, eventually mauling us 5–0. That defeat had a crushing effect on us and, just before Christmas, we surrendered 2–1 to Celtic in the League Cup Final.

We had reached the final of the Scottish Cup in every season Greigy had been at the helm and now we faced our eighth successive SFA final. Old foes Aberdeen once more stood between us and winning that trophy. In truth, we should have won the game but Eric Black scored deep into extra time to condemn Rangers to yet another barren season.

I had played just twenty-eight games and had scored eleven

goals. I was closing in on my thirtieth birthday and I no longer had it in my power to lift Rangers off the floor. Those in charge at Ibrox decided my time had come.

12

LONDON CALLING

John Greig was my teammate and friend and he'd been my manager for five years. The look on his face made it perfectly clear it was all over for me under him at Rangers. It was August 1983 and Greigy was attempting to inject life into the sleeping giant that was Glasgow Rangers. I felt for John. He loved the club like few folk ever have but he was battling on many fronts now – not just against Celtic but against the emerging forces of the New Firm, Aberdeen and Dundee United.

The season just ended had promised so much but, again, it had finished with us winning nothing – an all-too familiar story since John had taken over from Jock Wallace back in 1978. Rangers had ended the league campaign a massive eighteen points behind the champions, Dundee United. We had reached the finals of both domestic cups only for it all to end in tears. The League Cup Final was lost 2–1 to Celtic and a Scottish Cup Final that should have been ours, against an Aberdeen side that was there for the taking, disappeared late on in extra time as Eric Black scored the only goal of the game.

I had been at Rangers for more than twelve years and now John Greig was edging me towards the exit door. The rot had set in the previous April when Colin McAdam, Gregor Stevens, Gordon Dalziel and I were put up for sale. It was made clear we were no longer wanted which, given the service I had put in, rankled with me. Playing for Rangers was all I knew and I told John there was no way I was going. When he became manager, I could have walked out and gone to a big club in England but my loyalty to him, the club and the fans saw me turn my back on those more lucrative offers.

However, the goalposts had moved. Rangers were sliding farther and farther down the slope and, as one of the last survivors from the halcyon days, it was only a matter of time for me.

Greigy pulled me aside before a reserve game at Falkirk. 'Listen, Derek, I still want to change things and I don't see a place for you this season,' he said. I don't think those words came easily to John. We had been close but he was now a boss under pressure. He was desperate for a spark, something to get Rangers going, and so past relationships went out the window. I understood his position but I was not for moving.

He had a carrot, though. 'Chelsea are coming to watch you tonight,' he said. 'I think they are very keen on taking you to London. It could be a good move for you and a fresh start.'

I knew all about Chelsea's interest as they had been sniffing around for some time. The manager, John Neal, had a Scottish number two called Ian McNeill and he had been sent to see if I still had something in the legs.

At that time, Chelsea were in Second Division, one league below the top flight. They had long been one of the establishment clubs in England and were still viewed as the most fashionable in London, even though they were not in the same division as city rivals such as Arsenal and Spurs. Stars such as Peter Osgood and Charlie Cooke had turned Chelsea into a side people liked watching. Like Rangers, they were desperate for success and, as Ian McNeill was to tell me, this season was to be the start of something big.

I talked it over with my wife Marion. It was a tough call as it would mean upping sticks with our three young daughters and moving to London but I knew my time at Rangers was over. Within a few days of the Chelsea scouting trip north, a £30,000 fee was agreed between the clubs and there was nothing left for me to decide. On 1 September 1983, I signed for Chelsea.

The Johnstone clan settled in the small market town of Tring, a lovely wee place about thirty miles outside London in Hertfordshire.

On my first day at Chelsea's Harrington training ground, I had my first chat with my new manager, John Neal. He had been busy in the transfer market and wanted to build a side capable of getting out of a tough league that included the likes of Newcastle, Man City, Leeds and Sheffield Wednesday. For big games, it was not unusual for Stamford Bridge to house crowds around the 30,000 mark. Now Neal had to deliver promotion.

'It's good to have you here, Derek,' he said. 'I know you've had a good career up at Rangers and won a lot but I'm being up front with you – I see you as cover for the strikers I have. If Kerry Dixon or David Speedie get injured, you'll be the back-up.'

To be fair to Neal, at least he was honest and put me in the picture. I had known, deep down, that would be the case as Speedie and Dixon were the younger models – quick players with a real eye for goal – but it was a challenge. If you ask any player, they'll tell you they always feel they can get into the team – even if Maradona is occupying their position!

The training at Chelsea was of a very high standard. Over the next couple of weeks, I became fitter than I had ever been and my weight got down to an all-time low of around twelve and a half stone.

At the Bridge, we had a wee Scottish contingent of me, Joe McLaughlin, wee Pat Nevin, Speedie and a promising young Scottish striker named Duncan Shearer so settling in was never a hassle. I knew the score and I just trained away and played as many games as I could in the Combination Reserve League to keep myself sharp.

While things could have gone better on the field, off the field was turning into a real bundle of fun. The two biggest characters in the Chelsea dressing room were the Welsh duo, Joey Jones and Mickey Thomas. Both of them were all-rounders – they liked a bevvy, a night out and a good laugh. Their sense of humour was infectious and, on top of that, they could play. Along with the likes of emerging talents such as Nigel Spackman, Clive Walker and Eddie Niedzwiecki, they were forming a Chelsea side that had serious title aspirations.

'So, big man, how are you settling in?' wee Mickey asked me, a couple of days after I had arrived.

'It's going well,' I told him. 'The family like it, it seems a decent club and they look like a good bunch of lads. How do you find London yourself, wee man?'

'Oh,' he complained, 'it's fine for a right good night out but I wouldn't want to live here.'

'What a cryptic answer,' I thought. I had seen Mickey and Joey arriving together at training each day and then leaving Harrington in the same car. I naturally assumed they stayed near each other in some part of London. London? They didn't even stay in England! It was Kerry Dixon who told me they still commuted from Wrexham on a daily basis – a staggering three and a half hours each way. It was akin to Kenny Dalglish playing for Liverpool, while still living in Glasgow. But Mickey and Joey refused to leave Wales which is why they were known as 'The Nomads'.

Given their logistical problems, it was not unusual for the Blues Boyos to organise alternative accommodation of an evening, especially if the lads had a night out. They would cut a deal with the physios and get the keys to their treatment room and, when we came in for training next day, Joey and Mickey would be snuggled up under a blanket on the physios' beds. It was hilarious.

John Neal was quite comfortable with what went on because he was getting results as the battle raged for the 1983/84 English Second Division title. However, I was finding it impossible to get any kind of action with two sub appearances my total contribution. I was loving life with my new teammates and the bright lights of London and the West End booze-ups organised by the Scots lads were great but they were small consolation for not playing.

It was November when I was called to John Neal's office. 'Would you be interested in going back to Scotland for a loan spell, Derek, just so you can get some games and stay sharp?'

I almost froze on the spot. Jock Wallace was back at Rangers after Greigy had finally succumbed to the pressure and quit in October. Did the big man want me back?

Neal intruded on my dream. 'It's Dundee United,' he said. 'There is a chance for you to go and play there for a month.'

It was my hometown team, my boyhood heroes. How could I say no? Jim McLean was the boss at Tannadice and he had just turned down the chance to go to Rangers. So, too, incidentally, had the boss of the other half of the New Firm, Aberdeen's Alex Ferguson.

I had heard good things about McLean from my brothers, who were all still big fans of United, the reigning champions at that time. I decided it would be a good move. I would get games at a higher level as I approached my thirtieth birthday and I could fulfil that childhood ambition to pull on the Tangerine.

I had hardly checked in at Tannadice when one of the United coaches, with a broad smile, told me to put 19 November in my diary.

'Why's that?' I asked.

'That's the day you're going back to Ibrox to play against Rangers.'

Christ! The thought had never crossed my mind. When Greigy made it clear, after I'd spent twelve seasons at the club, that I had to go, I had never dreamed of one day playing against Rangers. But Ibrox it was and, as it turned out, it would be Jock Wallace's second game in charge in what was his second spell at the club after he had left Motherwell to take over from Greigy.

If going into Ibrox and seeing all the old faces felt weird, having to change in the away dressing room was even weirder. In fact, it was one of the strangest days of my life and it was the only time in my football career when I was happy to be named as a sub. It would have suited me fine not to get on that day.

Midway through the second half, wee Jim sent me out to warm up. As I trotted past the east enclosure, the fans gave me a tremendous reception and it was the same when I warmed up at the Copland Road end. It was very emotional. I had always shared a good relationship with the fans and I hadn't had the chance to say a proper goodbye to them.

My head was obviously messed up as I made my way back to the dugouts and plonked myself down on the bench.

'Fuck off!' said a voice beside me. 'You don't play for us any more.' You could never mistake that Jock Wallace growl.

By force of habit, I had returned to the home dugout. As I hastily obeyed – with a parting smile and shake of the head from Big Jock – and sheepishly made my way across to the visitors' dugout, the punters roared with laughter.

Within a couple of weeks, I was back at Chelsea, who were motoring in the league race. It had been six years since the fans had seen their team in the top flight and there was a growing feeling this could be the year. Neal had them playing some lovely stuff. The goals were flying in and the camaraderie off the field was paying huge dividends on it as the players homed in on promotion.

As we headed into the spring of 1984, the title race was between Chelsea, Newcastle and Sheffield Wednesday. Going into the last day, we were ahead on goal difference and we had to win at Grimsby to be crowned champions. John Neal organised a double-decker bus for the players and all the staff. When we arrived at Grimsby at around 1.30, there were already 6000 Chelsea fans packed into the Mariners' Blundell Park ground.

As the players walked across the pitch, getting a feel for the surface, wee Pat Nevin bowed to the crowd and tipped his white fedora. They loved it. The wee man – who would later be named Chelsea's Player of the Year – was one of their favourites. He was always a bit off the wall, was Pat. On Friday nights before games, he would head up to Manchester

Colin Stein chases the ball as Bobby Moore, Martin Peters and I look on during my debut against England at Wembley in 1973

A bow before Her Majesty in the 1977 Silver Jubilee game when a Glasgow Select played England at Hampden

Sharing a break from Scotland training in Troon with Celtic pals Kenny Dalglish and Danny McGrain

A typical header as I bullet the ball home against Northern Ireland at Hampden in the 1978 Home Internationals

Rod Stewart pops into our hotel base in Dunblane to record the Scotland squad song before the 1978 World Cup in Argentina

The open-top bus ride around Hampden before the Scotland squad headed off for Argentina – some fans really thought we could be the competition winners!

A new role required a new hairstyle – at the beginning of season 1978/79, I reluctantly became Rangers' captain

At last! We beat Hibs 3–2 in the second replay of the marathon 1979 Scottish Cup Final

A rare success as the lads celebrate thrashing Dundee United 4–1 in the 1981 Scottish Cup Final replay

I'm being closely marked by Borussia Dortmund's Ralf Loose in the 1982 UEFA Cup first-round match at Ibrox, which Rangers won 2–0

I get a hug from 'The Bear' in a typical Roy Aitken tussle in our April 1982 2–1 defeat at Celtic Park

Me and the girls – my ex-wife Marion with (from left to right) Heather, Judith and Donna in 1984

Home again – Jock Wallace brings me back to Rangers from Chelsea on 18 January 1985

Behind my desk at Firhill as I take over as Partick Thistle player-manager in the summer of 1986

Catwalk kings! I lead Colin Jackson and the late, great Jim Baxter out at the launch of the new Rangers kits in 1996

Commentating on another Old Firm clash at Parkhead with my old pal Hugh Keevins in 2002

The Arrochar clan at my tribute dinner in the Glasgow Thistle Hotel in February 2007

Walter Smith, Sandy Jardine, Willie Johnston and Ally McCoist joined me at my tribute dinner

or somewhere to watch bands no one had ever heard of. He's still an eccentric today, kidding all you TV viewers he knows the game!

It was a tense afternoon at Grimsby but Kerry Dixon's thirty-fourth goal of an amazing personal season was enough give Chelsea the Second Division Championship. Although I joined in the celebrations, it's always hard to feel the same elation when you have been a fringe player. I had hardly kicked a ball for the first team and, even though I was very much one of the lads, it wasn't like winning titles at Rangers. However, my mood changed when the one and only Ken Bates entered a frenzied dressing room half an hour after the final whistle. The controversial Chelsea chairman put his hand in his jacket pocket and pulled out a wad of notes that would have choked Steptoe's horse. It was around £2000 and he threw it on to a table in the corner of the dressing room. 'Buy as much fucking champagne as you like – you are the champions!' he shouted. The boys needed no second invitation.

We headed for the car park, running the gauntlet of thousands of jubilant Chelsea fans before we could reach the double-decker, which they were rocking from side to side. Eventually, we made good our escape, nicking down a couple of side streets before stopping at a convenient off-licence. Armed with Bates's booty, some of the boys piled off and returned with an obscene amount of champagne.

The journey home passed quickly but not quietly. We were all thoroughly pissed but in magnificent voice. All the lads had parked their cars at the Bridge so we helped one another off the bus and calls were made to wives and pals to pick us up. Meantime, the champagne kept flowing.

I was delighted for the manager and the players. OK, I

hadn't contributed but being a part of a dressing room that wins something is always special. I headed off for the summer with a lot to think about. Chelsea were into the top flight with the elite of the English game but was I going to feature against those sides if I hadn't been able get a game in the Second Division?

On the plus side, the money was good and the lads were great. The family had settled well in Tring and I did not really want to uproot them all over again so I decided to give it a few months into the start of the 1984/85 season to see how things went, rather than make any rash decisions.

John Neal strengthened the side again over the summer, knowing it would be a different ball game in the First Division, and one of the new faces he introduced to the dressing room was to prove familiar.

'I know we have a lot of Scottish lads at the club,' he said and, smiling at me, added, 'but our latest signing is especially for you, Derek.' With that, in walked big Doug Rougvie.

I almost collapsed. It was lost on most of the lads in the dressing room but Doug and I had enjoyed something of a stormy relationship from his time at Aberdeen. We had clashed on several occasions, most notably the 1979 League Cup Final. Off the ball, he had gone right through me from behind but the referee, Ian Foote, spotted it and big Doug was sent off. We went on to win that final 2–1, which was my first trophy as Rangers captain. I was accused of diving, which was absolute nonsense. I think the referee later confirmed in a book I had done nothing wrong and big Doug was totally to blame when the red mist descended.

I've heard people suggest that the problems that still exist today between Aberdeen and Rangers stem from that incident but I have to say I don't agree – a certain incident involving Neil Simpson and Ian Durrant may be nearer the mark.

Anyway, I extended a hand to my new Chelsea teammate and, to be fair to big Doug, he shook it warmly but we were never mates at Chelsea – too much had gone on between us.

A couple of years ago, I met Doug in a Glasgow restaurant with Andy Watson, the former Rangers No. 2 who was his mate from their time together at Pittodrie. We enjoyed another warm handshake but this time we had a beer and a laugh and it felt good to make peace with one of my old adversaries.

Doug started well at Chelsea, crunching into Viv Anderson with one of his bone-jangling challenges in the season opener, a 1–1 draw at Arsenal. We then went on to secure a similar scoreline against Man United but, by this time, my opportunities were even more limited.

I was restless. Marion knew it and it was time to make a move. A familiar place was calling me and it was to prove too much for my heart to resist.

13

RETURN TO REVOLUTION

The threatening growl on the other end of the phone had guaranteed my complete attention so many times. Jock Wallace had barracked me and he had praised me but now he was offering me a return to Rangers.

Chelsea was just not working out – it never really had. I had slipped into my thirties, the clock was ticking on my career and I didn't want to be stuck on coaches travelling to the middle of nowhere for second-rate games watched by two men and a dog.

Rangers had never been far from my thoughts and I knew they were toiling badly. Jock had answered the SOS from the board and, after a bit of a wrangle, he had left Motherwell to replace John Greig. I don't think Jock could ever have said no to Rangers, even if he hadn't been first choice. In truth, he wasn't even second choice as Jim McLean and Alex Ferguson had both turned the job down but they didn't have the history or the affinity with Rangers that Jock had. The club was well and truly in his blood. That was what drew him back – that and the fact he had quit in 1978 when he probably didn't want to.

Such an emotional tie to any club is hard to deny. Look what happened when Sir David Murray went back to Walter Smith and Ally McCoist after the Paul Le Guen regime fell apart.

Rangers meant everything to Jock Wallace and watching them slip farther into the mire would have been killing him. He knew I shared that affinity and the way he was trying to entice me back no doubt mirrored exactly what had happened to him when Rangers came calling.

It was January 1985, halfway through the season, and I was desperate to be back playing. Jock was looking to change things a bit, spur the team on for the second half and add to the League Cup victory that had come courtesy of a 1–0 win over Dundee United. He felt I could still do him a turn and I wasn't about to argue.

My fitness wasn't bad – the strict, hard training regime at Chelsea had seen to that – and I still had hunger – but gnawing away at me was the thought that trying to recapture my halcyon days at Ibrox might be the wrong move. I had been part of a special era but things had changed – Rangers were on the slide and the standard of player had dropped.

I talked it through with Marion. If she agreed, it would be the second time in just eighteen months the family would be uprooted. But she left the final decision to me – she knew how much Rangers meant to me. So I had a word with John Neal and the clubs agreed a fee of £20,000, which meant Chelsea had lost just £10,000 on me. On 18 January 1985, I re-signed for Rangers.

Up until the turn of the year, the league championship had been a three-horse race between Aberdeen, Celtic and Rangers. But Rangers then lost the Ne'er Day Old Firm game 2–1, drew with Dundee and lost to Hibs. It was a disastrous start to 1985 and my first game – the day after signing – was to be against the league leaders at Pittodrie. In all my time at Rangers, we never had it easy in the Granite City. Aberdeen were going strong and had a good side – if we wanted to have any chance of hanging on to their coat-tails, then victory would need to be secured.

In the event, my second debut for Rangers was a disaster. Aberdeen thrashed us 5–1, with Frank McDougall scoring a hat-trick. They ran over the top of us, much to the delight of the locals and our title bid more or less died there and then. The bus journey back was one of the quietest I've ever experienced. I just sat there thinking, 'What the fuck have I come back to?' I had not been on the end of many sore faces in my time at Rangers but this had been a real doing.

Needless to say, on the Monday, Big Jock stormed into the dressing room and read the Riot Act. He had been lucky – he had missed the game while recovering from a hernia operation and the unfortunate Alex Totten was the man in charge. But that didn't stop Jock leaving no one with a name and rightly so. It was just not good enough for Rangers to be losing 5–1 away from home. But this was a side in decline and I had been given my first, close-up view of it.

Two weeks later, I scored the first goal of my second stint at the club in a 2–0 win over Morton but tragedy was just around the corner. Gates were dwindling. The fans were seriously unhappy and who could blame them? The results were a disgrace and this team was taking Rangers into their darkest hour.

The Scottish Cup was our only chance of silverware. For our fourth-round tie against Dundee, just over 26,000 of them turned up at Ibrox and they didn't like what they saw. In the ninth minute, a certain John 'Bomber' Brown scored the only goal of the game. He was beginning to emerge as a talent at Dundee and would later succeed in getting his dream move to Rangers, his boyhood heroes, but, right there, he inflicted a killer blow on Rangers' 1984/85 season. How that must have hurt Bomber!

I had managed twelve appearances and had only scored that solitary goal. More worryingly, things were going exactly as I had feared they might. Had it been a mistake? Was I going to taint the memory of everything I had achieved here?

Rangers were once more a shambles. The man who had led them to two Trebles in the 70s may have been back at the helm but his squad was falling well short of the standard expected. And it was no longer a case of battling with just Celtic because the New Firm, Aberdeen and Dundee United, had come to the fore and Rangers were now the fourth force in the land.

With every new season comes a fresh wave of optimism and the summer of 1985 was no different. As always, Jock ensured his players would be exceptionally fit by leading our annual crusade to the sand dunes of Gullane to prepare for what lay ahead.

The Rangers fans were possibly at their lowest ebb in all the time I had been associated with the club. The last title win had been in 1978 and, bar a Scottish Cup win and a couple of League Cup successes, there had been little to cheer in seven years. No wonder the support was ebbing away.

I had settled back into life at Rangers and in Glasgow. Being that bit older than my first time around in the 70s, I took in much more of what was going on and I also listened a lot more to the fans. They were crying out for something to happen. The stadium was there and it was a splendid one at that – it was the envy not only of every club in Scotland but also of many clubs throughout the UK.

Just about everything Rangers had tried to do to awake this sleeping giant had failed. They'd made managerial changes and brought back the old warrior Jock Wallace to try to recapture the old days. The fans longed for the day when they could go to Ibrox and enjoy themselves again but they were being served up some second-rate stuff. I sympathised with them and knew they deserved a lot better.

When I was playing in the 70s, I used to get fed up with stories about the famous Ritchie, Shearer and Caldow team from the 60s. We had made our own stories and become heroes in our own right by winning a European trophy and two Trebles in three seasons. So, when I was asked by the press and fans about the state of the current crop and what had gone wrong, it didn't feel right for me to be going on about my 70s side. The team I had come back to was a million miles away from the 70s but it was my job, just as much as it was the manager's, to try to get the team going again.

Guys like Bobby Russell, Davie Cooper and me, we were all hurting for sure. We had played in good Rangers sides and we sat down with the manager at the start of the new season to try to get the team into some kind of shape for what lay ahead.

Jock called me into his office a few days into pre-season training. This hulk of a man, again carrying the full weight of expectation of a struggling club on his broad shoulders, was visibly getting older. I looked at him and saw the strain. He had been back at Rangers for a while now and the ship was still rudderless. I wondered how much more he could take or, more to the point, how much more the board would take.

Rangers were owned by the US-based Lawrence Marlborough. He was beginning to take a far bigger interest in what was going on and, when he appointed the forward-thinking David Holmes as chairman, I think Jock started to feel he was drinking in the last chance saloon.

'This club means everything to me, Derek,' said Jock, as we sat together before the season started. 'It breaks my heart to see these fans getting nothing back. We have to try and get Rangers back to being a force. This club is an institution.'

I could tell from the tenor of his voice that this was maybe something Jock felt he could not achieve. He needed big money to buy a better quality of player but that cash wasn't forthcoming.

As always he showed concern for others. 'I'd like you to get involved in a bit of coaching over the coming season,' he said. 'I don't know if you will start as many games as you would maybe like but, if you drop down into the reserves, I want you to be the coach out on the pitch. We have a lot of younger ones coming through and they will learn more from you than from someone shouting at them from a dugout.'

I liked the sound of that. I hadn't thought about what I was going to do long term in the game but I was approaching thirty-two and half my life had been spent in football – and top-flight football at that. I didn't know how much longer I could go on playing and the idea of getting into the coaching side of things did appeal.

Realising that I hadn't brought what he'd hoped I would to the team, on my return from Chelsea, maybe it was Jock's way of letting me down gently. We had been doing the equivalent of trying to turn back a clock that had no hands.

The season started well, with five wins from the opening six matches and Ally McCoist was beginning to score goals. I had always liked the look of this lad. He had everything and, on my return from England, I had seen something special. In all my years in the game, I don't think I've ever seen a more natural striker. And I played with some players who would have cost many millions these days. His instinct in the box is something I've never seen in a player since. He was hungry – boy, did he want it! He fought tooth and nail to be a Rangers player and was one of a very few diamonds in the rough.

Jock's summer demands appeared to be bearing fruit. He was also changing as a manager and, instead of just laying down the law as he had before, he was welcoming discussion among the players. 'I don't want bitching sessions – just be honest about the guy next to you,' he would say. That led to some bust-ups on the training ground, as is the way when players' egos are at stake, while others would simply take the huff.

We might have begun the season well but there was still this lingering fear that the walls would come crashing down and, sure enough, after our bright start in the league, we won just two of our next ten matches. Once again, the fans wondered what the hell was happening. The only highlight was on 30 November when Celtic were thrashed at Ibrox during a game in which Ian Durrant, Coop and Ted McMinn starred as a strong Celtic side was crushed 3–0.

The Skol Cup, as the League Cup was now known, had again looked good. We were winning it so often they should have given it to us to keep. After beating Clyde, Forfar and Hamilton Accies, a semi-final against Hibs provided the opportunity for yet another date at Hampden Park. A large crowd packed into Easter Road for the first leg. They saw Alan Rough save a penalty from Coisty then, inside eight second-half minutes, Hibs scored twice.

I had been struggling with fitness and I was also desperately short of form. We were into early October and I think my appearance at Ibrox in the second leg was just my third outing of the campaign. A crowd touching 40,000 turned up to see if we could turn things around. It was another massive show of support and loyalty from the troubled legions but again they were let down. On the half-hour mark, Davie Cooper cut the deficit to just one goal but we could not get another and Hibs ended our two-year reign as holders.

In Europe, Rangers had achieved little since the bright nights of the 70s. We were drawn against Spanish unknowns Osasuna, who would be making their debut in Europe when they came to Ibrox. It was a rain-lashed September night for the first leg and I am convinced the game would never have started had it not been a European tie. The rain was the heaviest I have ever experienced and I was only a substitute. In the dressing room at half-time, rivers of water were running out the door from the amount of water pouring off the players. It was a scandal, really but, if the game had been postponed, UEFA may well have struggled to get another date before the second leg and so it went ahead. Craig Paterson scored with a header but we felt that was not enough, given that we had enjoyed the lion's share of the ball.

Two weeks later, we travelled to northern Spain. I returned to the starting line-up for a game that summed up just how fragile we were as a team. Jock had sent us out with the firm instruction to keep things tight. Inside twelve minutes, we were one down and by half-time it was 2–0 in a game where we could hardly muster an effort on goal – yet another familiar story, yet another disaster.

By the turn of the year, as we headed into 1986, we sat fifth in the table, five points behind top-of-the-table Hearts, who were making a serious tilt at the championship. Dundee United were second, with Aberdeen and Celtic behind them.

This time, the Ne'er Day game at Parkhead ended in another

defeat for us with Celtic winning 2–0 and, there and then, the fans decided they had suffered enough. The Skol Cup was gone, the UEFA Cup run had ended and now the most painful experience for any Rangers supporter – defeat to Celtic – had dealt another thudding blow to any title dreams.

Three days later, as we hammered Dundee 5–0 at Ibrox, fewer than 14,000 fans turned up and who could blame the stay-away thousands?

Jock Wallace was seriously feeling the heat. Nothing he tried was working and the annual summer change in personnel had brought little in the way of either stability or ability. Looking back, I think the problems Rangers encountered around that time were very similar to what has been happening at the club over the past few years. There were changes to the team, maybe too many, and we had our moments, the fleeting good perform-ances, but the quality was just not there. You can never win things if you don't have a decent group of players who know what it takes to be winners at the Old Firm – guys who can cope with the demands.

The Scottish Cup presented us with the only chance of silver-ware and the draw could not have been worse – Hearts at Tynecastle. The Edinburgh men were flying at the top of the table and had some good players in a very decent side – Henry Smith in goal, Sandy Jardine, Craig Levein, John Colquhoun, Gary Mackay and wee John Robertson up front.

Despite taking the lead through Ally McCoist before half-time, Rangers lost 3–2. Wee Robbo scored Hearts' winner with five minutes to go and our season was over. A four-team battle was raging for the 1985/86 title – and all that was left for Rangers was a slog for a European spot.

Jock was gutted. Seldom had I seen him so low. We all

knew something had died that day and in his heart Jock must have known he was on borrowed time. Season after season, the slump had been going on for far too long and the club had become a laughing stock. In the eight seasons since Jock had guided Rangers to the Treble, we had won no more titles and, during the same time, just four League Cups and two Scottish Cups had been presented to Rangers captains – six trophies from the twenty-four up for grabs was a damning indictment.

It finally dawned on the decision makers, too. They had, no doubt, been sitting around the Ibrox boardroom table, muttering, as Ally MacLeod had done, 'It will come, it will come.' In the event, it did come and from a very unlikely source.

On 6 April, I left Ibrox after yet another defeat – Spurs had come north for a friendly and had beaten us 2–0. As I drove home, I mulled over what the headlines might be next day and I was thinking that, by this time, the press must be running out of negatives. But nothing could have prepared the players for the events of the following day. Word came down to the dressing room that Jock had gone. He was no longer manager and a major announcement was imminent. Players can gossip with the best of them and the speculation was rampant. Unlike today, when stories are leaked to the media before any official announcement, we had no hint of the tidal wave that was about to hit Rangers FC.

Graeme Souness was named player-manager on 7 April 1986. He had been playing with Sampdoria in Italy and it would cost £300,000 to buy out his contract with the Serie-A side. It was one of those moments when, genuinely, words fail you.

I had always admired Graeme Souness. Of all the players I'd come across, he was up there among the top five winners.

He hated losing at anything and he had that mean streak to go with it. I had known him since our days with Scotland and I knew he was a big Rangers fan. We had chatted about the club and he was always keen to know what was going on. I would never profess to be his pal. Our relationship was strictly as Scotland teammates and we'd maybe have a bit of a catch-up if we came across each other at some football function. He was a man who had built a world-class reputation with what he had achieved at Liverpool . . . and now he was the manager of Rangers? I couldn't get my head round it.

As the dressing room buzzed with what life would be like under the Souness regime, I knew many of the guys around me would not survive. This was the start of something huge and Souness would come in and take this bull by the horns – it was the only way he knew.

It was an exciting time to be at Rangers but I knew I was coming to the end of my own spell and would struggle to stay on in any capacity – even though a part of me hoped that Graeme may well give an old Scotland teammate a chance.

Because he had to see out a month or so in Italy before taking over, Alex Totten was in charge of our game at Clydebank the weekend after Graeme's appointment. We had to win to stay in with a shout of a UEFA Cup place. We lost 2–1. With the shadow of Souness hanging over them like the sword of Damocles, many players in that Rangers team preferred to sign their own death warrants. The first acts of the revolution were played out the following week.

Walter Smith was named assistant manager with immediate effect, signalling a quick end for Totten and coaches John Haggart and Stan Anderson. I knew Walter well. He had played at Dundee United and was so highly regarded at Tannadice that he had been groomed by Jim McLean as his assistant. He was also a massive Rangers fan – he would have walked from Tayside to take the job! Walter's appointment was instantly regarded as a shrewd move by Graeme. He may have known all about Rangers but he was out of touch with the Scottish game and Walter had the inside track on every team and every player. More importantly, he also knew Rangers. A case can be made for saying that Walter Smith was Graeme's most significant signing.

The press were speculating that Graeme would get a right few quid to spend and I also thought that had to be the case. There was no way a man of Souness's reputation would have taken the Rangers job had he not been given assurances that big money would be there for investment. It was the only solution to the problems bedevilling Rangers.

Walter's first game as caretaker manager until Graeme's arrival was at St Mirren on 19 April. The build-up was over-shadowed by the disappointing outcome of the first flexing of muscle by the new regime at Ibrox. Rangers had bid £500,000 for Dundee United's highly rated defender Richard Gough and the Tannadice club had rejected it. I had to laugh when I saw the headlines about the attempt to bring Goughie to Ibrox as, years before, he could have been signed and sealed by Rangers for nothing.

I could recall this skinny South African kid appearing at the old Albion training ground one bitter winter's day, having been recommended for a trial. He was only about five foot nine – not yet big enough for centre-half material – and, though he looked good enough on the ground, he got battered about a bit. John Greig said he wasn't interested and Richard Gough ended up at Dundee United.

So this was Graeme Souness's first major transfer swoop. Rangers had been reluctant to spend money but here was a clear sign the board had bought into their manager's rebuilding project.

Perhaps it was the transfer speculation that affected the way the team played at Love Street. Were some players worried that they might be dropped when Souness came in? With a European place at stake, such was the importance of victory that Walter promised a triple win bonus but even that didn't work. We crashed to a 2–1 defeat. Walter swept the dressing room with a look of disgust. I thought to myself, 'I bet he's asking himself what the fuck he's got on his hands here.' He was reporting back to Graeme, assessing who had a chance of surviving the axe and who didn't and few were doing themselves any favours.

There were two matches left to play, Aberdeen away and Motherwell at home, and points had to be bagged to get us into the UEFA Cup. A 1–1 draw at Pittodrie was the penultimate result – and then the man arrived.

I went into Ibrox as normal for training and sensed from the moment I pushed open the front door that something had changed. People were marching around, looking a lot busier than usual. Not a lot was being said but it was very business-like.

Graeme Souness' first address to the squad was quite general. He was in charge, he was the boss, no grey areas on that. But we had a big game against Motherwell and everyone had to focus on that to make sure we got the win we needed to ensure a UEFA Cup spot. With Graeme in charge, it was no surprise that we got the result. A 2–0 win brought down the curtain on our season and some worried players waited for the axe to fall on them.

Souness was about to head off with Scotland to the 1986 Mexico World Cup Finals. He had no time to mess around – he needed his plans set in motion.

Celtic had snatched the title from Hearts on a dramatic last day, winning on goal difference after thrashing St Mirren. We had to play them in the Glasgow Cup Final at Ibrox. It would be the perfect opportunity for the Parkhead faithful to rub our noses in it. There might have been a little bit of concern on the other side of the city about the threat posed by the arrival of Souness but Celtic were in a position of prolonged dominance over us and we could not get much lower.

Graeme sent for me on the day of the game, 9 May 1985. He was in the ref's room and had been calling the boys in one by one. Dave McKinnon, Eric Ferguson and Billy Davies had all been freed and wee John MacDonald and Dougie Bell were up for sale. I think these 'interviews' were a Souness ploy to get the whole place on tenterhooks. If you hadn't been tapped on the shoulder you would bust a gut against the newly crowned champions that night in the hope you were safe.

As I sat down, Graeme said, 'It's good to see you, big man.' The thing about him was that he always looked teammates straight in the eye, none of this eyes wandering around, hitting the floor. With the press and people he didn't know he rarely had that eye contact but Graeme always seemed more at ease with fellow players.

I wondered if our past relationship with Scotland would count, or maybe he had been told I was showing an interest in coaching. Was there an opening?

'What do you think about the state of this club?' he asked. 'You've been here, seen it, done it. Be honest with me.'

'It's a sleeping giant, Graeme,' I said, returning the compliment

163

and looking him straight in the eye. 'For this club to be in this position is just not acceptable and I'm glad you have taken the job. It's a big task but Rangers are a huge club – the biggest in Scotland. Someone needs to shake them up.'

'I agree,' he answered, dipping his head ever so slightly. 'I'm here to make Rangers the best team in this country and I will. Nothing will stop me from doing it – I have the resources and I am going to bring this club off the floor.' And then he added, 'But I'm sorry, Derek, I don't see any part for you any more.'

I had known it was coming. I'd hoped he would be upfront with me and he had – that was no flannel. I wasn't privy to all the plans but I knew Rangers were about to awaken from their slumber. Souness had that look – the one I had seen many times, the one that said he wanted it big time.

We chatted for a few more minutes and he got up and shook my hand. 'I want you to come in tonight – come and see the Celtic game,' he said.

I was pleased he asked me. I think he recognised what I had given to the club and he didn't want to throw me out like a pair of his old boots.

At home, when I told Marion the news, I think I was still in a bit of a daze – most of the lads who'd been told the same thing probably were.

I wanted to see the Glasgow Cup Final and so did more than 40,000 punters who'd showed up – such a huge turnout was the first sign that the Souness bug was beginning to bite.

The Celtic fans partied in the Broomloan Stand – the champions milking the moment. Meanwhile, deep inside Ibrox, a certain Ally McCoist was sailing close to the wind with his new boss. Coisty's contract was up for renewal but he was one of the players we all felt would be safe. Despite being in a poor side, he was banging in the goals and had the makings of a top striker. Graeme knew that too but he had pencilled in Coisty for his interview before the match.

As usual, Ally was running late. He burst through the front doors maybe an hour before kick-off and Graeme was majorly pissed off. He told Ally he would speak to him later and to get himself stripped smartish.

I think that was the first hint that the boy from East Kilbride had someone writing his scripts. After infuriating his new, no-nonsense boss by turning up late for talks, the bold Coisty went out and blasted a hat-trick as Rangers won the Glasgow Cup 3–2. I sat in the Main Stand and smiled. If Coisty fell in the Clyde, he would come out with a pocket full of goldfish.

Graeme assembled everyone in the dressing room and I mean everyone – the squad who had just beaten Celtic, the players who had been freed, those up for sale, the coaches, the whole shooting match. 'Tonight, you have given something back to your fans,' he began, 'but that's all. With all due respect, the Glasgow Cup means fuck all. You heard the away stand tonight – well, take that away with you. Go away and rest and come back ready and prepared. You will be working harder than you ever have – I will set standards you have never seen. There will be some major players coming to the football club. Across the city, they can have their moment. From next season, we will be taking it back.'

All eyes were on the man who had just spoken. Graeme was still in his early thirties and still playing but, in his first mana-gerial role, he already was assuming the mantle of a veteran boss.

I said my farewells to some of the lads, to the doormen and the staff and, as I walked out of Ibrox for the last time as a

Rangers player, there was one almighty lump in my throat. I walked slowly across the dual carriageway to the school where my car was parked and I resisted the temptation to turn for one last look at that famous old red brick façade. Tears were already very close. At the age of sixteen, I had come to this place to chase my dreams and, except for the eighteen months I'd spent at Chelsea, this was all I had ever known. I cried all the way home.

I had no bad feelings towards Graeme. He did what he had to do and he did the right thing. My day had gone and it was about the future now. If you believed his words – and I did – then Rangers were about to rise like the phoenix.

The daily diet of what was happening at Ibrox kept my mind off what the future held for me. I wanted the best for my club, to see them back at the top. When Graeme started bringing in the likes of Terry Butcher and Chris Woods, the England captain and their goalkeeper, I was as excited as the next Rangers fan.

Scottish football was never given time to prepare for the Souness revolution. He blazed a trail for a quality of import never before seen in our country and blended them with the best we had to offer – the likes of McCoist, Cooper and Durrant.

Rangers won the league title and the Skol Cup in his first season. He grabbed our game by the scruff of the neck and shook it until the rest started to respond. I knew he would do it. He told me so the day he said it was over for me at Rangers and, when Graeme Souness said he would do something, it normally got done. He was, without question, the catalyst behind the club as it is today.

Souness took Rangers to a different plane. He started the influx of top players, the foreign buys, the big transfers and the wages that even teams in England couldn't match. And we should not forget, either, the foresight of David Holmes and a Rangers board led by majority shareholder Lawrence Marlborough for enticing him there in the first place.

Celtic had to respond but Souness had stolen a march. Up until 2000, when Martin O'Neill arrived and the cash dried up at Ibrox, I don't think Celtic recovered from the start Souness gave Rangers.

He also brought David Murray to the club and, no matter what opinions the Rangers fans have of their current chairman, no one can question his colossal contribution. When Murray bought control of Rangers in 1988 he proceeded to chase all our dreams. His rightful place and that of Souness in Rangers' history will never be forgotten. It broke my heart to leave but I knew my club was in a safe pair of hands.

14

JAGGY THISTLE

Ken Bates peered out from behind his thick, tinted glasses and it was impossible to tell his expression. Knowing him, it was probably devilment. It was a muggy June afternoon in 1986. My playing days had ended the month before when Graeme Souness brought the curtain down on life at Ibrox and, as I approached my thirty-third birthday, I had been cut loose from the only life I had ever known.

This meeting in a Glasgow hotel had been arranged during an intriguing call from Bates, the colourful and controversial former chairman of Chelsea. I had got to know him during my short stint at Stamford Bridge. He had just taken control of Partick Thistle and he had a proposition for me.

His arrival had predictably sparked fears for the future of the Firhill club. The press suggested he would use Thistle as a feeder club for Chelsea, while he countered that he had big plans and claimed that the third team in Glasgow would soon be challenging the big two. It would be interesting to hear what he had to say.

'How do you fancy joining Partick Thistle as a player-coach?' Bates had wanted to know on the phone. 'You are a legend at Rangers, you have a great profile and I think you can help with the plans I have for the club.'

I had reservations about both roles. Firstly, I had concerns about my fitness – my knees and ankles were shot, as had been proved during my disastrous return to Rangers. Frankly, after sixteen years of almost non-stop football and more than 540 games, I did not think there was much left in the old tank.

'But you'll be dropping down a level,' said Bates, giving it the hard sell. He was doing everything he could to persuade me to take the leap into coaching.

As every ex-pro will tell you, it's hard having to contemplate the end of your playing career and never again pulling on the boots and crossing that white line. Bates pressed the right buttons on that front. I was letting my heart rule my head – my body had told me it was over but I couldn't let go.

As for the coaching – that also troubled me and with good reason. I have often been a big critic of the so-called 'Largs Mafia'. Anyone who wants to become a coach in Scotland has to complete the SFA courses down at Inverclyde. I've gone on record as saying these courses don't produce managers – they simply develop robots. But, as I was to find out to my cost, I was lost without technical knowledge and Largs, for all that I don't rate it much, would have at least given me some of that.

Bates told me that money would not be a problem. I had been on decent wages under Bates at Chelsea and he knew roughly the pay packet I had been picking up at Ibrox. He put a cracking deal on the table and, to swing it, I was given the extra incentive of a company car. Considering I had just left Rangers a few weeks earlier, this deal would give me some financial security. Also, I thought, I could hop on the first rung of the coaching ladder, which may well lead to openings in the future.

But one other anxiety for me was the fact that this offer was

169

coming from Bates and not the Thistle manager who, at that moment in time, was the great Lisbon Lion, Bertie Auld.

'I assume I am going to be a coach working under Bertie and that I'll still play a bit?' I asked Bates.

'Of course, Derek, that is the plan. I just feel that, with your reputation, it can work. It will be great for Thistle having a big name like yourself on the staff.'

I liked Bertie. He had been a real winner on the pitch with Celtic and he was a good guy off the pitch as well. But when he got wind of what I had been offered, especially the club car, he was raging. It was understandable – he was the manager at Thistle but the guy who was to be his number two was coming in on a better deal. I don't know if Bates had it planned that way and my deal was designed to get Bertie out the door but Bates must have known it would upset Bertie. He was the board's man but Bates had come in over the top of them and he wanted his own people. I was a pawn in the endgame – Bates wanted me as manager – and, two days after I had agreed to become player-coach of Partick Thistle, Bertie chucked it.

'Derek, I want you to be the manager,' said Bates. 'It's a fantastic chance for you and I'll support you all the way.'

To be honest, I didn't want the job. I was probably the most reluctant managerial appointment in the history of the game but Bates was persuasive. I flagged up my concerns about members of the Thistle board not accepting me because I was his man but he said dealing with them would be his problem. So there I was – Derek Johnstone, player-manager of Partick Thistle and the start of the 1986/87 First Division season was just around the corner.

The first thing I did was to bring in John Hagart who had

been a coach at Rangers. He had tremendous in-depth knowledge of the game and was good in terms of training and tactics. He was also the kind of guy players would respond to. Fitness was also one of his strengths. In a league where it was dog eat dog, if I could get the Thistle players lean and fit, then I felt that would maybe give us an edge.

They were a great bunch of lads and I could never question their desire or commitment but there was a dearth of talent in the pool. We had some journeymen but we had no quality. Despite suggestions that Bates would put a few quid on the table for new players, there was nothing to spend. A transfer budget did not exist and it was a case of trying to make the best of what we had. I began to fear that it could be a long season.

I didn't settle well into the managerial hot seat. When you are a player, the only person you need to worry about is yourself. You train, play games, go home, pick up the wages and that's it. You might have the occasional press interview or represent the club by appearing at a function but, in truth, players have a fairly easy life – and players these days have it even cushier. So, suddenly, there I was with responsibility for twenty other guys and I found it really hard to cope. I had to get training organised with John, pick the team, look at deals for getting guys in on loan or for free and handle the daily calls from the press. Looking back, I probably realised very early on that being a manager was not for me but quitting isn't in my nature.

Thistle have always had a hardcore of loyal support. To this day they turn up and follow their team and I think they do have their own special place in the heart of Scottish football. Maybe it's simply because they are the alternative in a city dominated by the Old Firm but their fans are a good bunch and they got right behind us as the season began under the new manager.

It could not have been any worse. After seven games without a win and defeat in the Skol Cup at East Fife, I was feeling the heat big time. The players had their limitations but that doesn't wash when results don't go to plan. I was the boss and I was taking the flak from the stands and also from sections of the boardroom.

From down south, Ken Bates was keeping a watchful eye on how things were going but certain directors resented the fact that I was his appointment and the bad results were giving them plenty of ammunition. One director firing his share of the bullets that were coming my way was Jim Donald. He was perhaps better known for his connection to Ashfield dog track but now he was questioning the fitness of the players and the effectiveness of my methods.

I confronted Donald about what he'd been saying and he was quick to have a go. 'The players are not fit enough,' he said. 'I think I am fitter than some of them.'

Now, I knew some of our players were not the best but to say they were not fit enough was a slight on John and me. 'Is that so?' I responded. 'Well, tell you what, if you think you are fitter than some of them, let's put it to the test.'

I never expected him to take me up on my offer – he was a member of the board, for goodness' sake, and he was no spring chicken. But, no, in front of an amazed squad, Donald took to the Firhill pitch to join in our running exercises or, as they are known on training grounds across the land, doggies. Within a couple of sprints up and back, up and back, he was blowing out his arse. It was maybe a stupid way to prove a point but, as he puffed and panted his way back to the dressing rooms, I felt I had at least made my point about fitness.

I may have won that small skirmish but it looked as if the war was being lost. Results were not improving and I was not enjoying it one little bit. Of course I wanted to be a success but some people are just not destined for certain things in life. Far better players than me have gone straight from the dressing room to the dugout and failed as managers.

However, through it all, the players gave me everything – including the bizarre. There was a reserve game at Firhill – one of those nights when you're lucky if three men and a dog turn up to watch. We had a big centre half named Alan Mackin. He was later to become manager and chairman at East Stirling, while his son, also Alan, became a very successful tennis player. Anyway, Alan was getting pelters from this guy in the wee enclosure in front of the main stand. I told him to ignore it but, in an empty stadium, every word can be clearly heard. As the game moved into the second half, the abuse got worse. 'You are a big arsehole, Mackin,' the cretin shouted. Further words were exchanged and the guy signed off, saying, 'I've seen you in that big fancy fucking Mercedes, Mackin. I'm gonnae tan it.'

When the final whistle blew, Alan raced off the pitch, showing an impressive turn of speed I hadn't often seen in training or in games. He belted up the tunnel and out the front door, still in full Jags strip and boots, and spotted the guy loitering at his Merc. Well, let's just say this guy didn't hang about. As we all piled out into the street outside Firhill, there was Alan chasing this guy down to Maryhill Road. As I said, bizarre.

The details of what happened after that are a bit sketchy but it was the end of Alan's Thistle career. The board wanted him out and he went that night. The last thing I needed was to lose another player. We had got a lad up from Chelsea called Colin West, who had banged in a few goals and added a wee bit of quality, but the knives were being sharpened in the board-room and the fans were not at all happy with what they were seeing.

Because of injury problems, I had only managed to play in four games and, by the February, I called Ken Bates and told him I wanted out. The team were eighth in the league and I could not take them any higher. As I've said many times since, I think Thistle were ninth the season before so at least we made progress!

I was owed some money as part of my deal and, when it was not forthcoming, I decided to keep the club car until I was paid. Billy Lamont had come in to replace me and I wanted everything settled up so that I could get on with my new job, which was at Radio Clyde.

It was while I was covering a Saturday game for Clyde, up at Tannadice, that the company car disappeared from the driveway of my home back in Glasgow. The neighbours told me how one those big tow trucks rolled into the street just half an hour after I had started broadcasting on Clyde from Dundee. It mounted the kerb, smashed over a rockery and on to my front grass. The metal arm was quickly up and moving and the Partick Thistle club car was heading down the street within five minutes.

It was a sour end to my brief sojourn with Thistle. I did finally get paid after some talk of legal action, but it didn't need to end like that. And – surprise, surprise – Bates did not follow through on any of the grand plans he had outlined and he, too, was soon on his way.

That came as a relief to the fans, who rightly feared for

Thistle's future. And the club did manage to go on and achieve some success, which I was pleased about.

The Firhill board, to their credit, have had some real Thistle guys in charge for a long time – men who fought long and hard to bring the club back from the brink of going under. But they have been a yo-yo club. The only man to get them going has been John Lambie. He's been manager three or four times and *is* Partick Thistle. They have had loads of managers but none can touch Lambie. I couldn't make it work and neither could the likes of Sandy Clark, who only lasted a short while as well. A few years ago, Derek Whyte and Gerry Britton took over. That brought back memories as they had moved from playing straight into management. Again, they struggled. Since my day, Thistle have had around a dozen managers. At the time of writing, Ian McCall is the latest incumbent and I wish him well.

Thistle have little money and they will always find it hard against clubs who have wealthy owners or a better infrastructure. For all the woes I had there – and it was probably the longest eight months of my life – I still look for their results every weekend.

I have had a few wee tickles from clubs wondering if I might want to get back into management at some level but that one stint at Firhill was enough for me. I vowed never to go down that road again and that, at least, was the right decision.

15

ON TO THE AIRWAVES

I had started doing a bit of work for Clyde towards the end of my time at Rangers. I had always got on fairly well with most of the press guys and understood they had a job to do. They had to dish out stick at times and, as long as it was constructive, I had no problem with what they did.

I love talking about football. I was reared in a dressing room where the craic was second to none. The big shy kid who had turned up from Dundee had to learn quickly and much of my personality was formed through interacting with the characters I came in contact with during my early years at Ibrox.

Richard Park, Dr Dick, was top man at Clyde and, when I wasn't playing, he'd get me in to do some sports desk chat, commentate on games and offer up analysis and opinions. When I left Rangers, he asked me about joining the radio station full-time but I opted for the Partick Thistle job instead. After that brief sojourn, I was keen to get into the broadcasting side of things. I also had a living to earn.

Sports programmes in Scotland were boring – and, I have to say that I include both Radio Clyde and the BBC in that statement. Richard and Paul Cooney, who was emerging as the sports anchorman, believed we should provide more entertainment for the punters and they felt I had something to offer in terms of not only my insight but also my sense of humour.

I loved going to games and commenting on them. It was all about opinions and still is. The biggest problem I had was trying not to say 'we' and 'us' when I was working on a Rangers game. Richard reminded me I didn't play for Rangers any more and had to appear impartial. 'Christ,' I thought, 'this is going to be hard.' I didn't have a contract – in fact, it was only twelve years ago that I finally signed anything with Radio Clyde – but I really took to the airwaves and loved the job.

The station was beginning to take off. We designed it basically for listeners in West Central Scotland – the Old Firm, really – although that has changed and its audience is now more widespread. The major breakthrough came with the introduction of the Radio Clyde Open Line. Richard and Paul reckoned that, after games, most fans would take at least an hour to get home in their cars and buses and they would love to hear other punters, maybe those who had got home faster, phoning up to have their say on the action they had just seen. Everything was open to debate – whether it was the referee, their own team, the opposition or even us. It was a tremendous idea and it became a phenomenal success – to such a degree that every other radio station in the country, and a few on the telly, finally copied us.

For the first time, fans had their own platform and it took off big time. It sparked incredible debate and had all sorts of arguments raging every Saturday. It was underpinned by the late great Jimmy Sanderson. 'Wee Solly', as he was affectionately known, was one of the most respected sports writers in the business – and he could have started a barney in an empty house! Jimmy would come out with such classics as 'Bunkum!'

when he disagreed with a caller and he would sometimes ask them waspishly, 'Were you at the game, caller?' He loved to be controversial. It was all part of the act and, boy, did it get the lines buzzing.

Gerry McNee followed in Solly's footsteps by using the same style of barking out controversy designed to get the punters going. And now we have our very own Hugh Keevins doing exactly the same today. The thing about all three men was that they gave their opinion. If they took pelters for that, then so be it. They were man enough to have a go and they took it back.

The Open Line has been going for twenty years and is still the most listened to slot on Radio Clyde. But it was not without its teething problems. After reporting on a Rangers v Motherwell game with Chick Young – before Chick's Bosman to the Beeb – I had chosen Richard Gough as my man of the match. Minutes later, a guy calling himself Stevie phoned in from Govan, and asked to speak to us. 'Derek, I think Andy Goram was man of the match today – he had some good saves,' said Stevie, who we assumed had got home quickly from Ibrox, given his address.

'No, I don't agree, Stevie,' I replied. 'I didn't think he had much to do, really.'

'Nah, he was the best player on the pitch,' said Stevie.

Wee Chick said, 'Well, we have the former Rangers captain here, Stevie, and he thinks Richard Gough was the top man. Are you sure you were at the game?'

'No, I wasn't at the game.'

'So, you're coming on here and saying Andy Goram was better than Richard Gough and you didn't even see the game?' said an exasperated Chick.

'Aye, that's right,' said our caller. 'What do you want me to do? Sit at home and say fuck all?'

The Open Line has an eight-second transmission delay. If any caller, such as our ex-pal Stevie, swears or says anything outrageous, we can fade them out using what's known in the business as a 'dumpy button'. If you hear a radio presenter saying something along the lines of 'It looks like we've lost that caller', then it's more than likely because they have said something that would have had Ofcom on the blower first thing on the Monday morning.

That's the kind of nonsense we have to deal with on the phone-in – that and call after call on exactly the same subject and making exactly the same point. But the vast majority of the punters are great and love their football and they make Glasgow unique.

Football is king in Scotland but Paul and I would cover all the action from any important sporting event on our lunchtime sports desks. I particularly remember the time when Croy's Pat Clinton was fighting for the European flyweight title in Cagliari, Italy, in August of 1990. 'Derek, we can't end this lunchtime sports desk without a mention for Scotland's own Pat Clinton,' said Paul. 'The wee man is fighting for the European title and it's bound to be a great night when he goes toe-to-toe with the Italian, Salvatore Fanni.' That surname had no sooner left Paul's lips than he was grimacing – well, he knew my sense of humour.

'Absolutely, Paul – all the very best to wee Pat. Who did you say he was fighting, again?'

If looks could kill . . . 'Salvatore Fanni,' Paul repeated, trying to keep a straight face but dreading the inevitable punchline.

'Well, that's a very unusual one, isn't it, Paul? You don't hear of many people in these parts called . . . Salvatore.' Done like a dinner!

We worked so well together. Paul was a master at bringing

everything together and, with his excellent timing, he knew just how to use live radio to get those kind of laughs.

One of the major bonuses of being a sports reporter at Clyde was getting to cover the major European club matches and the Scotland games. In my playing days at Rangers, nothing came close to the buzz of a huge game against Continental opposition under the lights at Ibrox. But the buzz I got from working at those games was great, as well.

Going to World Cups and European Championships was also fantastic. I started at Italia '90, then covered the European Championship in Sweden in 1992, Euro '96 down south and then France 1998, which was the last time Scotland qualified for a major tournament.

Some of the guys on the *SuperScoreboard* team – the younger ones, naturally – have yet to experience such tournaments and that is a real shame but then some fine Scottish players never made it to the finals of a big competition, either.

At the World Cup in Argentina in 1978, I would watch the press guys scurrying around for stories. They all had demands and deadlines and all the players had to do was make themselves available. To be fair, good tales were not in short supply at that particular World Cup! But, when I jumped to the other side of the fence, I saw how hard it can be.

It's fine on the days when things are set up in terms of press conferences – that is a piece of cake – but, at France '98, we had to fill three slots a day for Clyde – breakfast, lunchtime and drive time. And, at times, it was hard to sniff out wee tales – the snippets that would keep the fans back home involved. The games took care of themselves but it can be hard work covering a major tournament. In saying that, who wouldn't have wanted to be in my shoes in Paris, the Stade de France, Brazil v Scotland in the opening game? Those are the kind of doors that working at Radio Clyde has opened for me and it's been great.

I've always tried to be as diverse as possible in my media work and at all times to give an honest opinion on whatever topic has been put in front of me. When I started at Clyde, I was asked to do some work for the *Evening Times*. I'd always enjoyed a good relationship with their sports guys, quality writers like big Alan Davidson, and it was one paper that was always fair and balanced (yes, they have a Celtic columnist, too!). I started with a letters page, answering the readers, and then I was given my own weekly column. I'm not going to spin you the line that I write it myself. Whichever one of the lads is ghosting the column gives me a call and I have a chat with him, just like you'd have with your mates, about the day's hot topics.

I still have my weekly *Times* column (at the time of writing, anyway!) and I love doing it. It's unusual for a paper to have kept the same person for so long so I must be doing something right. I think the paper is happy that people buy it to see what I'm saying. It's the same with the *Rangers News*, where I also have my column. With so many great ex-Rangers players out there and a few guys that younger fans might want to hear from, I take it as a great compliment that my opinion counts enough for people to want to employ me.

A few years back I took a stab at TV work. I had enjoyed doing voice-overs on the various Rangers end-of-season DVDs down through the years and I always felt fairly comfortable in front of the cameras. My name was put forward to STV to present *Football First*. It featured the First Division and went out on a Sunday with all the highlights from the previous day's games. I swithered for a while, as I was happy at Clyde, but in the end I did the screen tests. Although there were around eighteen people up for the presenter's job, it was offered to me.

I thoroughly enjoyed the show. It was never done live so I had to get used to reading from autocues, which was hard. I got a bit of stick from my pals for it but I thought I did not too badly. When we had a guest on, we could chat off the cuff and I felt most comfortable with that because I could feed off the answers and develop the conversations more naturally.

It lasted a while and then changes took place at STV and they got staff guys to do it but it was something else on my CV. I was glad I took that wee venture on but radio is what I enjoy most and working for Clyde has given me some great memories – and some high drama.

I didn't think the climax to the 2003 SPL championship could ever be beaten in terms of excitement but I was wrong. Four years ago, Celtic came back from the agony of losing the UEFA Cup Final in Seville to play Kilmarnock at Rugby Park on the final day of the season. Rangers hosted Dunfermline at Ibrox and were ahead in the title race only on goal difference.

It was an unbelievable day. The goals flew in at both grounds but the title was not settled until the final minute of additional time when Mikel Arteta stroked home a penalty to make it 6–1 for Rangers. It was live radio at its very best and, two years on, no one could believe it was actually being bettered.

Peter Martin is a great radio anchorman. In the Paul Cooney mould, he's brilliant at capturing football's drama and excitement and he wrote his name into the history books in 2005. Going into the last day of the season, Celtic were two points clear of Rangers. They faced Motherwell at Fir Park and Rangers were at Easter Road.

There had not been the same build-up as there was in 2003

as any surprise outcome would have been much more of a long shot. It was just expected that Celtic would do the business. So, when Chris Sutton put Celtic ahead, it looked to be all over even though Nacho Novo had given Rangers the lead at Easter Road and that was how the score remained for most of the second half.

I was in the studio with Peter and Davie Provan, watching both games coming in on two TV screens. Whenever the three of us think back to the games' astonishing climaxes, we still shake our heads today.

Scott MacDonald – ironically now a Celtic player – equalised for Motherwell with a minute to go and, before anyone could draw breath, the wee Aussie striker had clipped home a second goal to rob Celtic of the title and gift-wrap it for the Ibrox side. I fell off my seat with excitement and almost choked on the microphone cord. Peter then uttered his now classic line, 'The helicopter is changing direction!' That was a reference to the SPL chopper which, at that moment, was doing a mid-air U-turn. Having been headed for Fir Park to present the trophy to Celtic, its pilot had to change course and head for the capital.

Talking of U-turns, I have been advised to take a few of them lately. It stems from a conversation I had in January 2007 with prominent people at Rangers, who assured me they had shaken hands on a deal to sign Scott Brown from Hibs at the end of the season. They had bid for both Brown and Kevin Thomson, Brown's fellow Hibs midfielder. Thomson did move to Ibrox for £2 million but the club was told they would have to wait for Brown. The player, it was repeated, had shaken hands on a deal and everything had been agreed. This was reported in various newspapers and, because of this, I said on the radio, many, many times, that I felt he would definitely be going to

Rangers and a lot of other people said the same thing. Maybe I was more forthright than most in predicting what would unfold but I wasn't afraid to stick my neck out and I was in good company – my old pal Keevins was saying the same. So, when Scott Brown signed for Celtic in a Scottish record 4-million deal, no one was more surprised than me!

I was slaughtered on the radio, with some callers demanding I resign, as I had said – jokingly – I would fall on my sword if it didn't happen. I got it wrong. All I did was pass on what I was told to my listeners but I needed to learn from that. And I did learn one thing – money talks. Rangers believed they had the boy and then Celtic came in and blew them out the water with the transfer fee. Hibs sat back and watched the price rise – quite rightly from their point of view – and Rangers walked away.

If Rangers had matched penny for penny what Celtic had tabled, Scott Brown would be a Rangers player now. But they didn't so choosing between the two clubs was never an option for him. Sometimes you just have to hold your hands up and admit you were wrong. I did and I would do the same again if I got something wrong. It's part of the job.

My Clyde colleague Davie Provan – at one time, a fellow-columnist on the *Evening Times* – gives you it straight as well. Everyone knows that Davie enjoyed a terrific career at Celtic but his connection with the Parkhead club doesn't stop him saying what he feels. He gives his views without fear or favour and I think that is what earns you respect. Davie knew what had happened with the Brown situation and he wasn't afraid to speak about it. That's why Radio Clyde is the best station in the country and leaves everyone behind time after time when it comes to ratings. We have the best sports show in Scotland with the best presenters, pundits and journalists.

ON TO THE AIRWAVES

I've enjoyed working with the likes of Paul, Peter, Hugh, Andy Walker, Fraser Wishart, Mark Guidi and Darrell. OK, we don't always get it right but we try our best to entertain and inform and I'd like to be doing it for another twenty years.

16

DAVIE COOPER DEAD

Davie Cooper was born to play for Rangers – he always believed that – and after watching him rip John Greig apart, I had to agree with him. It was the autumn of 1976 and we squared up to Cooper's Clydebank in the last eight of the League Cup, little realising the saga that lay before us.

In the first leg at Ibrox, I scored but that 3–3 was dominated by the performance of twenty-year-old Coop, who lit up the pitch and scored the goal that earned Bankies a share of the spoils. Coop gave Greigy a torrid time – something not many people did – and laid down his credentials for the big move that people were rapidly beginning to link him with.

In the return match at Kilbowie, Coop was once more awesome. Again he struck an equaliser after Greigy had given us the lead. The tie could not be broken and, at 4–4 on aggregate, we went to a play-off twelve days later. Amazingly, that game ended 0–0, taking the tie into a second play-off at Firhill. It was the fourth time in under a month the teams had met and, in every game, Coop had stood out like a beacon.

He was to find the net again in the second play-off but we eventually found an extra burst and won the tie 2–1 with a goal from Bobby McKean to take us into the semis, where we were trounced 5–1 by Aberdeen.

By the following June, Davie Cooper got his dream move when Jock Wallace paid Clydebank £100,000 for his services. Davie said a host of English clubs had wanted to sign him and there was more money on offer from some of them but he would have walked from Clydebank to sign for Rangers. 'I played for the club I loved' was a phrase he was to use often.

Coop was one of three arrivals into the dressing room that summer who were designed to give the place a wee shake-up. Bobby Russell and Gordon Smith were the others – all good prospects and all desperate to succeed. And it didn't take long for them to start making an impact.

There was a school of thought that suggested, when Bobby Russell played, Rangers played. Bobby was a fantastic player – very underrated, in my opinion, by a lot of people in this country. He was a cultured operator and would easily have adapted to the modern game. Gordon Smith handled the step-up from Kilmarnock without any problems, scoring goals regularly and forming a good partnership with me at the spearhead of what was a strong and talented Rangers team. And then there was Coop. He was, quite simply, the most naturally gifted player I ever had the good fortune to play alongside. He has to be up there with the top five all-time Rangers greats.

I have been asked many times over the years about the understanding and relationship we built up on the field and it's true he created a large number of goals for me in the six seasons we played together before I left for Chelsea. For any centre forward, Davie was a dream. He could find you in the box with uncanny regularity, swinging over some tremendous balls, and it was my job to get on the end of them. With him on one

187

wing and wee Tam McLean on the other, it was no surprise I ended the 1977/78 season with thirty-nine club goals and the title of Scotland's Player of the Year.

Davie's natural game was to dribble and get defenders to commit. He would go past the best in the business as if they were not there. He was mesmerising – at times, it looked as though he had the ball connected to that famous left footed with a piece of string. I would say that about eighty per cent of the crosses Coop fired into the box provided genuine chances for a goal. OK, not every one of them would end up in the net but his delivery was superb. He also had this fantastic ability to dig a cross out just when it looked as though he was losing possession.

In his first season as a Rangers player, I think he only missed one league game as we stormed to the championship, and then eventually our second Treble in three years.

Coop scored the best individual goal I have seen in any game, anywhere. It was his famous 1979 Drybrough Cup Final goal against Celtic, when he played keepie-uppie with the ball up three times and slipped past defenders into the box, before scoring. It was a moment of genius from a man who could make a football do things that most of us could only dream about. My God, looking at the modern game, what price would Davie Cooper have commanded in his prime?

The funny thing about that Drybrough Cup Final was that Sandy Jardine scored a screamer in the 3–1 win over Celtic. It was a goal fit to grace any Old Firm match but it's never talked about because Coop's outstanding effort was the lasting memory.

I think it was the best goal Coop ever scored although his rocket of a free kick against Aberdeen in the Skol Cup Final a few years later ran it close.

He was nicknamed 'The Moody Blue' by the press because he very rarely gave interviews and was seen as a bit of a loner. Nothing could be further from the truth. In many ways, he was a bit like Kenny Dalglish – another guy perceived as being dull and moody when talking in public. Davie had a fantastic ability to deliver one-liners. He was sharp, quick-witted and liked a laugh.

His greatest passion was the horses. He was never a massive gambler, maybe just fivers and tenners on a couple of trebles or a yankee, but sometimes the result of the 1.30 on a Saturday afternoon could determine how he would play come three o'clock or certainly what kind of mood he would be in.

He and Bobby Russell became very close. They both enjoyed a wee punt. In the dressing room, we had a portable TV and Coop would stand there in his pants, glued to the box, watching his nag. Sometimes he would roar it home, other times the scrunched-up betting slip would go flying across the room. And, whenever we were at a hotel before a big game, he would always have a few lines on. The boys would gather around the radio, as sometimes the meetings weren't televised, and we would have a real laugh waiting for his three or four results.

On a few occasions, he would win big – I remember he banked a grand with a treble – and he would be as happy as Larry. Davie Cooper was at his happiest playing for Rangers or watching a horse trying to get its nose in front to give him a return.

Coop and I often went down to Ayr races with Ally McCoist (you might have heard that Coisty likes a punt). I am not big on horse racing but I enjoy the fun of the day out – and the few drinks that go with it. One particular Ayr meeting had been a sore one for Coop, whose wallet was taking a pounding as we headed into the last race of the day. The three of us were in the bar and Coop was feverishly studying the *Racing Post* pages pinned to the wall.

'I got a tip for this race last week,' piped up Ally, giving me a conspiratorial wink.

'What was it, Coisty?' snapped Coop, desperate to regain some of the losses that had left him down to his last few bob.

'Christ, I can't remember, Coop. A trainer told a pal of mine. What was it again?'

'For fuck's sake, Coisty, how can you not remember a tip? Come on, think hard, this is important.'

'Coop, it's gone. I honestly can't remember. Come on, DJ, help me out.'

'Jesus, Coisty, how the fuck would I know? It was you who got the tip.'

'Coop, I've got it. Horse number four – definitely horse number four, in race six at Ayr. That's it, Coop!'

Davie swung round on his stool and his eyes flashed to the *Racing Post* on the wall. As his finger moved down the page, his eyes were eagerly scanning the fixtures until he'd found the sixth race at Ayr and then horse number four. 'For fuck's sake, Coisty!' He was shouting at the top of his voice. 'Number four? The fucking horse is called Amnesia.'

Ally and I were rolling about the floor but Coop was hooked and, before we knew it, he was halfway out the door to get a bet on this nag.

A couple of months later, The Three Amigos were back at Ayr shooting a video. We were having a right good booze-up in one of the hospitality boxes, in what turned out to be one of the best days out I ever had with Davie. It hadn't been a great day for me in terms of results but I hadn't lost much. In the last race, I picked out a real outsider and slapped on £20 at 16–1. Coisty and Coop slaughtered me all the way back up to the box. 'That thing has no chance, DJ – it's got to be up for the milk cart in the morning,' quipped Coop, as we popped another champagne cork.

Needless to say, my rank outsider romped home three lengths clear. The three of us were hanging over the side of the box roaring it home, knowing I was on to a win of more than £300. As the horse crossed the line, the jockey looked up at these three madmen and punched the air. I waved a champagne flute in his direction and shouted, 'Brilliant, wee man! Come up for a drink.'

We were still celebrating and counting my winnings, when there he was. The wee jockey had come straight off the horse and up to the box and he was in full riding gear and colours, with his goggles on top of his helmet. He was the height of nonsense. Three glasses of bubbly later, he was pissed – a victim of the jockeys' struggle against their weight. He was carried back to the paddock, I collected my £300 and we headed back to Glasgow for a right good boozing session.

It was March 1995 and I was at the Radio Clyde sports desk when the call came in from Paul Cooney, who was working with STV. 'Davie Cooper has collapsed,' Paul said. 'He has been rushed to hospital and he's in a bad way.'

I dropped the phone. I had spoken to Coop only a couple of days before and he was going off to do a kids' coaching video at Clyde's Broadwood Stadium. What could possibly have gone wrong there?

The lines were red-hot as we tried to get more information and then Coisty phoned me. He had spoken to someone in the family and the news was not good. Davie had suffered a massive brain haemorrhage and was in a very serious condition.

During our lives, we will all experience that overwhelming helplessness, that agony of impending loss and the impotent anger that makes us cry out, 'WHY?' Davie Cooper was thirty-nine, a couple of years younger than me. He was a very fit guy but now he was in a coma, fighting for his life.

It was a terrible time for his family. To the outside world he was Davie Cooper of Rangers but to them he was just their Davie.

Coisty and I went to the hospital, where pictures of me driving away in tears were caught by one of the TV stations that had camped outside. Coop was lying peacefully, connected to a mass of tubes. He was still his good-looking self but he was gone – I knew it and Coisty knew it. We did not hold back the tears. We left his family to their vigil and, within a few hours of our leaving, Davie passed away. A young guy, a hero for his clubs and his country in our national sport, he'd been cut down in his prime. The entire nation was stunned. The Rangers family had lost one of its favourite sons and, within hours, those huge wrought-iron gates guarding Ibrox had become a place of pilgrimage.

When the Celtic fans came together after the death of Jimmy Johnstone, it reminded me of the huge esteem in which our football heroes are held. Like Coop, Jinky was a genius – maybe even the greatest of them all. Losing such players – men who the fans feel they have come to know personally – stuns the supporters and drives them together in grief. *That's* what clubs like Rangers and Celtic are all about.

Coisty and I decided to meet up in Bridge of Weir and raise a glass or three to Coop. Sometimes hitting the bevvy is not the answer in these situations but we wanted to have a few and remember. It ended up an all-nighter and we laughed and cried.

Davie received a fitting tribute at Ibrox when the Cooper Suite was named in his honour. It's appropriate that, on match days, the players use that suite, a place named after one of the finest talents ever to play for the club they now represent.

Motherwell also suffered loss. Davie had moved there and been a star for them, helping them to success in the Scottish Cup. They named a Fir Park stand after him, which says a lot about that club. The people at Motherwell deserve tremendous credit for that. And when his two teams met in the 2005 League Cup Final – ten years after his death – it inevitably became known as the Davie Cooper Final.

Davie's first season at Rangers, 1977/78, had been marred by another tragic death. Bobby McKean had been with Rangers since 1974, having signed from St Mirren. He lived in Barrhead and would pick me up at my house in Dean Park on our way to training in the morning. One day in mid March he failed to show and I was cursing him as I grabbed a taxi up to Ibrox.

The gaffer, Jock Wallace, asked me where he was, knowing we lived close by and were in the habit of going out for a few beers from time to time. But Bobby's non-appearance was as much a mystery to me. The boss phoned his wife but Fiona didn't know where he was, either.

Next day, Bobby McKean was found dead in his garage. He had been at a party, come home without any house keys and gone to sleep in his car. It had been a cold night and he had switched on the engine for some heat. The fumes killed him. It was the day after his twenty-sixth birthday. Bobby was a great wee player. His death overshadowed the season but winning the Treble was a fitting tribute.

Football can be a great, mesmerising and passionate game that thrills us all. But life can be tough and footballers are not immune, as I found out with the tragic loss of two pals.

17

DICING WITH DEATH

The walk from the hotel to the Rangers press conference was only 400 yards but, with every step, it felt as though I was wearing diving boots. Drenched in sweat and struggling for breath, I staggered behind the rest of the press guys who were marching ahead to get on with their work.

It was August 1995 and we were in Cyprus in heat so searing you wouldn't believe it unless you'd experienced it for yourself. Rangers were twenty-four hours away from the second leg of their crucial Champions League qualifier against Anorthosis Famagusta. The match was balanced on a piano wire with Gordon Durie's goal scored at Ibrox a fortnight before all that was separating the sides.

I was there to cover the match for Radio Clyde with Dougie MacDonald but, as I tried to wipe away the sweat that was seeping into my eyes behind my sunglasses, the game was the last thing on my mind. I felt rotten – so bad I sought out the Rangers medical team. My heart was thumping and racing madly and I was struggling to catch a breath. I was given a pill and I gulped it down with two litres of bottled water before heading back to the sanctuary of the fridge-like air-conditioning in my hotel room.

For the first time in my life, I had panicked. It was the fear of the unknown. What was the feeling that had overcome me? What caused the racing of my heart and the burning sensation in my chest?

In the cold light of the next day, I was wondering what all the fuss had been about. After a good night's kip, I was in the commentary position for Clyde as Rangers got the 0–0 draw they needed to open the door to the Champions League. It was so hot in the wee box we had been allocated, that Dougie and I had to strip down to our pants to commentate. What a sight that was!

I was delighted for Walter Smith and his players when they got through on the final whistle and, as we sipped champagne on a bouncing flight home, the warning from the Rangers medical staff to get a check-up was completely forgotten.

Some five years later, the blistering sunshine of a foreign country did for me again. This time it was the delightful Dubai. I had been invited along with Gordon Smith, Murdo MacLeod and wee Chick Young to do some after-dinner speaking to the ex-pats, play some charity golf and appear at question-and-answer sessions with the punters. It was a great trip. They're all good lads and we were having a ball – and plenty to drink.

At dinner on the third night I ordered a spicy Indian dish, some kind of curry, but the chef had piled on the chilli powder. Christ, it was hot! After a few bites the sweat started cascading. I felt dizzy and faint and, worryingly, that burning, racing pain was back in my chest. It felt as though my heart was going to burst out of my chest, it was pumping so fast.

As luck would have it, a doctor I had known from when I was living in Johnstone, in Renfrewshire, was working in

Dubai with Emirates airlines. I went to see him and he had me admitted to the local American hospital right away. He was seriously concerned by my heart rate – but not as much as I was. God, after reading about so many people having heart problems, was it now happening to me? Could I be on the verge of a heart attack? As I said, it was that fear of the unknown.

The unknown treatment for me turned out to be cardioversion. It's where they zap your heart with electric shocks to slow it down. I also had a day and a half on drips and being monitored, while the rest of the lads were on the beach and having a good night out. What a nightmare! But there was a serious problem and I had to confront it – there would be no forgetting about the second opinion this time.

Back home, the BUPA medical cover I had with Clyde got me an appointment at the Nuffield with a top heart specialist. My condition was carefully and clearly explained. I had paroxysmal atrial fibrillation – which basically means my heart is prone to speeding up when problems occur. I would be on medication for the rest of my life to regulate it. It was not ideal but a lot better than having a full-blown heart attack that could have killed me.

Some triggers had revealed themselves. Hot food was now a no-no as it was too risky. Two- or three-day benders could induce it so I'd have to cut them out. If I stuck to the medication and watched what I ate and drank, I'd be fine. But I could have saved myself some grief if only I had set about putting myself on a major diet there and then. I weighed more than eighteen stone and the specialist warned me that carrying such a load was putting great strain on my heart. But some folk don't want to hear what's best for them, do they? They just carry on regardless. Even though I had been warned, I made no attempt to lose weight.

For a few years, everything appeared under control. There was the odd day when I would lose breath as my heartbeat rose slightly but nothing serious. And that remained the pattern until 2002. I was on holiday in Portugal and two or three days of overdoing it had me near to collapsing. The temperature touched the high 90s and my chest almost exploded. By this time, I knew the signs and I also knew what it would take to sort me out so two days of that holiday on the Algarve were spent in a private hospital being zapped. Well, the experts at the Nuffield had warned me.

After tinkering about with the dosage of my medication, I was back to normal. Or was I? For the first time, there was the nagging worry that maybe one day I would not be in time to get zapped.

I had made the calls to Billy McNeill and John Greig – two of the finest footballers this country has ever produced – when they had their respective heart problems but never did I imagine it would happen to me.

It was four days before Christmas 2005, and I had been invited by well-known Glasgow club owner and businessman James Mortimer – a good friend of mine – to join some Old Firm players at a press photocall for the opening of One Up, his new place in Royal Exchange Square. I was happy to go despite being told by the lads on the sports desk at the *Evening Times* – where I've had a weekly column for years – that Peter Lovenkrands would be there. I was in the middle of a very public row with the not-so-great Dane. I had slagged him off in my *Times* column and on Radio Clyde for being too inconsistent during his time at Rangers.

As chance would have it, Lovenkrands was in the middle of a rare purple patch of form at Ibrox and scoring a lot of goals. He had scored in a Champions League game against Inter Milan, when Rangers made history by making it into the last sixteen, and later slammed some former Rangers players – guess who was amongst them! – for not getting behind him. I had replied that a few good games was not enough and a bit of a slanging match had ensued. However, I had no problem posing with Peter at One Up for the press photographers. Unfortunately, I never got the chance.

For some time, there had been a gallon bottle of whisky sitting in the office of the sports desk at Radio Clyde. I had asked what was happening with it and no one seemed too bothered who got it. And, no, I didn't plan to drink it myself – I was a changed man! I felt it would be a nice touch, particularly at that festive time of year, if we handed the amber nectar in for the war veterans at the Erskine Hospital. A couple of phone calls later, I had arranged to drop in, meet some people there, hand over the bottle and then head up to Glasgow to help out James with his publicity shoot.

The temperature in Erskine Hospital was in very sharp contrast to the freezing morning outdoors. It felt as if the radiators were on full blast and, just minutes after entering the reception, I began feeling dizzy. When the sweats descended, I thought, 'Shit, here we go again.' But it felt different this time. We were heading up a flight of stairs on the way to see the veterans when I just keeled over. I was out cold. Fortunately for me, a man coming behind me managed to break my fall but, when I came round, I thought I was dying. 'Christ,' I thought, 'this is it!' I have never felt so bad in my life. It was like a spear had been thrust into my heart.

Erskine staff got me on to a chair and down in the lift to the back door. An ambulance was there and its driver was about to finish his shift but he helped me into the back of his vehicle and we headed for the Western Infirmary with the sirens going. The traffic heading into Glasgow was horrendous, as you can imagine. It was just before Christmas and the shoppers had the place deadlocked.

I was so sick, I needed two of those wee upside-down hats, as I like to call them, to contain what I was bringing up. As I lay back in the ambulance, I thought there was no way I would get to the Western in time – my number was up. The staff were waiting at A&E and I was rushed into what is known as the crash room – and, no, it's not a place for motoring housewives!

The nurses were great. They talked me through all the procedures and tried to keep me calm as drips went in and the oxygen mask went on. But the pain in my chest was getting worse as my racing heartbeat went through the roof. When I woke up, I was in the high-dependency ward. I had been given the cardioversion zaps to get my heart under control but it took a day and a half for me to stabilise.

The press had got wind of my plight and were phoning the hospital. Through my friends at the *Evening Times*, I sent out a message in an attempt to kill the speculation. Deep down, though, I knew I was now dicing with death. I had been here before and the same thoughts were going through my head. Would I survive another attack? Why was I prepared to live with this time bomb, when I had the ability to defuse it, at least in part?

I was off work for a few weeks. The lads on the *Super-Scoreboard* team at Clyde kept my spirits up every weekend with their wee mentions but now it was time to meet this problem head on.

It transpired that, at my age, perhaps medication was no longer the correct treatment for me. I needed a lasting alternative and it was to be provided by my new specialist, the very reassuring Alan Rae. An operation, said Alan, was the only answer to what was a dangerous heart condition. This was no sooner said than it was done and I went into Ross Hall Hospital one Saturday morning in February 2006.

It was the same procedure as the one performed on Tony Blair (yes, our ex-prime minister has a heart, too). The operation is called radio-frequency ablation. A wire is inserted through the groin (steady, chaps) and moved up to the heart. A track is burned right across one of the chambers in your heart to prevent it from speeding up. During the procedure, I was sedated but not unconscious and I was discharged later the same day. At the time of writing, that was eighteen months ago.

The operation was a success but I knew I could not go back to my old ways. Of course, I had said this before, after a previous attack, but Alan Rae's warning, that he was seriously concerned about my heart, struck a chord. I had become – for me, your original lanky lad – incredibly fat. I was more than eighteen stones and, at my age and with my condition, that was medically negligent. So I went back to the old routine, in the gym, and I lost more than three stones. Because of my metabolism from when I was playing football, shedding the pounds happened quite quickly. No one could believe how thin I had become in such a short space of time. Some folk were worried about me. 'Are you ill, big man?' I was asked more than once.

Today, I feel great. I am happier within myself and I am

content in the knowledge that I have done everything I can to stay alive. Of course, you never know with heart problems – but, then, you never know with life.

18

FAMILY VALUES

Every man would like to look in the mirror each day and know for certain he'd done the best he could for his family but, sadly, I can't say that is the case with me. I have many regrets about some of the things I've done in my not-so-private life. My very public weaknesses – and also some lies in the press – have caused hurt and embarrassment to the people I love and hardly left me in a good light or feeling proud. I wake up every day and go to bed every night with that.

My ex-wife Marion and I have four lovely children, three girls and a boy. I love them all very much and, thankfully, even though I was not the best father as they were growing up, we all get on really well. The twins, Donna and Heather, were born in November 1979. It was the day before we played Valencia in the Cup Winners' Cup at Ibrox and I scored in a game we lost 3–1 and dedicated the strike to my two first-born.

It was funny. I had raced from training to the maternity ward to get my first glimpse of my babies, like any other doting new dad, but the sister wouldn't let me in. She only stepped aside after I had given her my autograph!

Judith came next, a couple of years later in 1981, and then my son Douglas was born in 1986.

My kids never wanted for material things when they were

growing up – they got most things they asked for. They lived in nice houses, had good holidays and they were happy. What they lacked was perhaps a more important item in their young lives – their father. I hold up my hand and say Marion did a fantastic solo job bringing them up. All four are a credit to their mother. Their dad was too busy being Jack the Lad.

I liked to socialise and rarely turned down an invitation. I would go out after training finished at twelve o'clock and have a drink with my pals. On a Sunday, I would head for an all-day shot and not appear home until after training on the Monday. I was hardly ever home. Being out on the town at all hours – a well-known young guy with a few quid in his pocket – I was a magnet for compromising situations and I didn't have the sense to resist. I was Derek Johnstone, the Rangers captain, and I lived my life like that a lot of the time. It was an unreal world but it was hard to step away from it and see what mattered most – my family. I made mistakes and Marion knew it.

I have spent a lot of time trying to make up for those lost years with my children. They were young and maybe didn't know what was going on all the time. But not coming home and staying out on the booze when I should have been the father they needed – that was out of order. And, having lost my own dad at a young age, I should have been even more aware of what I was doing to them. But sometimes you are just plain daft and think you only have to get up every day and worry about yourself.

Marion and I broke up in 1999. There is no doubt it was mostly my fault. I was no angel and I do deeply regret the hurt I caused. No woman would have accepted the way I was behaving and we just drifted apart. She had tried to get me to see sense but I didn't listen. She had stood by me through many bad times and she'd done her best to shield our kids from what was going on but I repaid her by acting like a fool.

We hung on and hung on until the kids were older and I suppose we did well to make our marriage last for the twenty years it did. Had it been the modern day, when couples split more readily, I think it would have been over much sooner.

Marion and I had met in Renfrew in 1976. We were introduced by mutual friends and got married in July 1978, after I came back from Scotland duty at the World Cup in Argentina. We were in love – no doubt about it. She was a smashing lassie and we got on great. She deserved much better.

We have been divorced for seven years and we've moved on with our lives. We are not the only people it's happened to and, even if in an ideal world it would be nicer for people to stay together, we have four kids and we continue to do the very best for them. I just hope they love their dad as much as they love their mum. As I say, Marion has done a wonderful job in very difficult circumstances.

My kids have made me very proud. Donna is a trainee accountant at the Glasgow law firm Maclay, Murray & Spens. She is married to Patrick and has provided me with my one grandchild so far. Wee Josh is four years old and is the apple of my eye. He is a cracking wee kiddie and I love spending time with him when I can. Donna is a very confident girl. I think she is the organiser among the kids and, as is often the case with twins, she is very different from Heather.

I really feel for Heather. She's had so many health problems down the years it's unbelievable – if there is anything going, she'll get it. The other kids are quite strong but she worries me. Heather took an active part in football and loved the game. She got involved in the coaching side and took classes at the local school in Houston. I had hoped she could maybe get into that side of the game and make a living but it's hard for girls even though she has three coaching badges and I think she has been a bit disappointed by that. She lives in the West End and plans to get married to Mark in 2009.

Judith was always a free spirit. She moved out when she was seventeen or eighteen, becoming the first to fly the nest. She is very independent and has always been single-minded in pursuing what she wants to do. She would take on a couple of jobs at a time to get the cash she needed to chase her dream, which was to be an air stewardess. She moved to the Isle of Man and got a job with Manx airlines but she's currently grounded. Judith and her partner Jay are looking forward to the birth of their first child – and my second grandchild – in the not-too-distant future.

And then there is Douglas. The way I treated him has left me with many more regrets. Douglas was thirteen when Marion and I split up and I left and it had a massive effect on him. We were the two boys together in a house of four women and we were very close. When things kicked off in the house, he always sided with me – as boys do with their dads. Of course, he was very much into football and he looked up to me. I would take him to Rangers games and he would sit up in the press box while I worked for the radio.

I watched him playing for his school and local boys' teams. He was a talented kid. He was strong and able to hold the ball up and with no little skill. Like his old man, he also had a bit of an edge to his game and I felt he had a real chance of playing professionally. I am not saying for certain he would have gone to the very top but I think Douglas could have followed in my footsteps and been a professional.

FAMILY VALUES

When his mother and I split, he lost interest. He didn't want to play football any more and that was my fault. I may have cost him the chance of a career in the game and I can never make up for that. I should have helped him – been there and encouraged him – but, the way things went, he drifted away from the game. Maybe he didn't want to chase the dream because he felt I had moved on and didn't care. But that was certainly never true – I always cared. Every day, I thought about all of them. But, for a boy, it's hard not to have his dad around on a day-to-day basis, especially at such a crucial time as the early teenage years.

As it is, he picked himself up really well. Douglas has a lovely girlfriend, Laura, and is in the final year of his joinery apprenticeship. He's a good boy and we get on well. We even went on holiday to Spain together last year and I really enjoyed that time with him. And I did get him his chance to play at Ibrox. T-Mobile ran a competition for fans to play on the pitch and Sandy Jardine and I were asked to manage the teams. I agreed on the understanding that Douglas could get a game. He was the captain, and scored the first goal as our team won 6–1. It was just a bounce game but it meant a lot to all the players who got that chance to play on the hallowed Ibrox turf.

Seeing my boy in a Rangers strip, playing at Ibrox, humbled me. I just hope he understands – that all my kids understand – that there are so many things I wish I could change.

Seeing me on the front pages instead of the back has not been easy for my family here or for the ones up in Dundee. My mother has had to see it all as well and it hurts her. She is always the first on the phone telling me to get my arse up to Dundee for a plate of her soup. I think she feels it can take the ills of the world away. It is great soup, though!

I am big enough and ugly enough to deal with the press. I know the way news reporters work and I can handle that, even if it leaves me baffled at times as to why they would be interested in me when there is so much else going on in the world.

I hit the headlines again around seven years ago when I started a relationship with Emma Dodds. At eighteen, she was much younger than me. We had met when she worked at Radio Clyde and we got on very well. The press claimed we had been having an affair when I was still with Marion but that was nonsense. Nothing happened between Emma and me until I was well out of the house and it was months before we became an official item. But that didn't stop the papers stirring it up because we worked together and because of the big age gap. They followed us for weeks to try to get pictures. It was hard on Emma and I felt sorry for her having to endure that kind of exposure. I told her it would all die down and it did. People maybe thought it wouldn't last but we fell in love and just got on with it the same as any other couple.

Emma was a great girl to be around – full of fun and life. We moved in together, had a good social scene and holidayed abroad just like everyone else. I was very happy but, as the years passed, I think the age thing began to tell. Emma had different priorities – those of a young woman – and I wasn't adjusting to these changes in our relationship as it evolved over the years. In the summer of 2006, we split up after more than six years together.

Again it was down to me but no one else was involved despite the press trying to dig away and see if there was. I was on the front pages again. Christ, there was a war going on in Iraq and major news stories were breaking all over the place but I got a call to say they had the story under the headline of 'Rocked

DJ'. For some reason, they found it big news that Emma and I had separated.

Reporters and photographers were camped outside Radio Clyde, for goodness' sake. They hid outside Emma's house and followed her to her pal's to try to dig up some dirt but there was nothing to find – we were just two people who had decided to go their own separate ways.

I called my kids right away when the headlines appeared. They knew things had maybe not been great between us for a few months but it's always a shock to see your dad's love life splashed across the tabloids. That has always been my policy with the kids. I phone them when anything appears and give them the truth. They are happy to get the explanation and, even though it can be embarrassing when their family and friends see it, they at least know straight from me what's going on.

Emma and I have remained friends. I learned a lot from that relationship – maybe more about myself than anything else. We had moved to a lovely house in Arrochar and, for a while after the split, I considered moving as it wasn't where I had come from. But it's amazing how things can turn out. I still stay in Arrochar, on a beautiful small housing estate, and I have made some great friends. My house is one of eleven and the development's builders, Jimmy and Alan Paterson, are great lads. They each have their own home in the scheme, as I call it. Their mother, Cathy Paterson, stays on one side of me and my neighbour on the other side is called Jenny. It's like being in a continuous episode of *Desperate Housewives*, living between those two!

Cathy hates it when we call it the scheme. I tell her that her house is the best hotel in Arrochar! I'm always in there and she makes me cracking dinners. Jimmy's son Lewis and his girlfriend Chelsay are often around so we have some great parties. Everyone takes a turn and I have a marvellous wee social scene.

I've also become friendly with the couple who own the Ben Lomond restaurant, Lynn and Donald Nicholson, and the owners of Loch Lomond cruises, Fred and Alison Moore and their kids Nick and Lucy. The folk up there could not have been nicer and I appreciate the way I've been welcomed into their community.

Arrochar is a great place to live and I've had a new lease of life. I love the lifestyle and, most days, I can nip down to the gym at Cameron House on my way to Radio Clyde. That has helped me get in shape and I feel much better about myself.

Things are going well in my personal life. I started a relationship with a lovely woman, June Lake, earlier this year and we have a great time in each other's company. I also enjoy spending time with June's three-year-old daughter Crystelle. Who knows what the future will hold? But, for now, I am happy and content.

My regrets over my family will never go away but I have to get on with my life and I'm trying to do that as well as I can. I have no plans to get on the front pages again but, with me, you just never know!

19

MY GREATEST RANGERS TEAMS

Many of the finest footballers Scotland has ever produced have donned the famous light blue of Rangers. Some of our country's best foreign imports have also graced the Ibrox turf, firmly establishing themselves alongside all the home-grown legends.

We all have our favourites – the guys we loved to see every week, the players who became our idols – and often it's a generational thing. I love the debate surrounding who's best and which players could possibly have spanned the generations and been able to perform in any era. It creates great arguments in pubs, clubs and supporters' buses the length and breadth of the country. So it was not an easy task to come up with DJ's Greatest Rangers Teams. Yes, teams plural – for one, I've chosen the best from my own playing days at Ibrox and, for the second, I've picked from what I consider to be the finest Rangers players I've seen since I stopped playing in 1986.

In my fifteen seasons at Rangers, I had the privilege of sharing a dressing room with some phenomenal talents and some incredible characters. It was tough choosing eleven from my former teammates and I apologise to any who may feel he should have got the nod – but it's my book. And wait till you see the opposition – a world-class, star-studded team chosen from the countless Rangers players I've watched since hanging up the boots. I'm sure you'll agree that it would have been a titanic confrontation, well worth the admission money.

So, with no further ado – and in 3–4–3 formation, which was favoured quite a lot back then – here is the best eleven from my Rangers career:

McCLOY; JARDINE, McKINNON, D SMITH; COOPER, GREIG, MACDONALD, W JOHNSTON; G SMITH, D JOHNSTONE AND STEIN

PETER McCLOY

What can you say about the Girvan Lighthouse? Peter was a fantastic Rangers keeper for sixteen years. At 6ft 4in, he was a giant of a man. He was very likeable off the field and always someone who would get involved with the banter and any nights out.

Like most keepers, big Peter had his moments – such as the time he was seen swinging from the bar in that Cup Final at Hampden – but he was a good, solid keeper and he organised the backline. He made important saves at important times as and, like many Rangers goalkeepers before and since, there were long periods in matches he would go without any action, as we were camped in the opposition half.

Peter also had the biggest kick-outs from hand I've ever seen – as was proved when he launched the ball 20 yards to set up wee Bud Johnston in Barcelona when we won the Cup Winners' Cup.

SANDY JARDINE

Sandy was the best right-sided defender this country ever produced. I know Celtic fans would say Danny McGrain was better and I agree that Danny was a top-class player. Scotland were very fortunate to have two top operators in the same position at the same time.

Sandy started off as a midfielder but was converted to a defender. He was quick – probably the fittest guy at the club during my time – and he could play. A real feature of his game was his overlapping runs and he swung over countless crosses for me and Steiny. Sandy could also pop up with a goal or two. He had a knack of finding the net in big games and he was a real Ranger.

I know he went on to Hearts and played until he was about fifty-eight but Rangers was always his club and, for me, he has to be in any greatest Rangers team.

RONNIE McKINNON

Ronnie was a no-frills defender who just did what it said on the tin. When Rangers were going through a hard time at the start of the Paul Le Guen era, they were crying out for someone like Ronnie to come into that backline and sort them out. His job was to pick up the danger man in the opposition strike force and Ronnie very rarely got caught out when it came to a battle with whoever that may be.

He was fearless and that meant that he picked up a few bad injuries – none more so than the broken leg in the Cup Winners' Cup quarter-final against Sporting Lisbon that saw him miss the final and create the space for me in the team.

Ronnie wasn't really an organiser or a shouter – he just went in and won the ball. He was an outstanding centre half.

DAVE SMITH

Dave was the finest sweeper this country has seen. I was delighted he was inducted into the Rangers Hall of Fame for his contribution to the club. What a classy player he was and I don't think he was ever booked. Dave was seriously under-rated. I smile when I read the kind of plaudits being lavished on defenders these days as some of them could not have laced his boots.

I had the pleasure of playing alongside him many times at the back for Rangers. He was a tremendous insurance policy and would say to me, 'Go and win your tackles, son. If you miss it, I'll sweep up.' And he did.

He could also come out with the ball from the back and create chances with his cultured left foot. Dave's reading of the game and passing ability were exemplary and he is a must for defence.

DAVIE COOPER

Coop started his career on the right wing and that is where he would line up in my team, coming inside defenders to use that dynamic left foot.

As I said in an earlier chapter, he has to be up there with the top five Rangers players of all time. He was a sensational talent, a guy who could get fans on the edge of their seats with his magnetic dribbling ability. Davie could also find you in the box with lethal accuracy and it made it easy for me to finish off a lot of those balls.

On the pitch, he was just a joy. Only a few players are blessed with that kind of natural talent but Davie Cooper was unique. People said he was moody and sulky off the pitch but that's just rubbish.

JOHN GREIG

I know Greigy played at fullback for parts of his career but I would have him occupying the midfield sitting role, which I always felt was John's best position at Rangers. He was the original Captain Fantastic – a Rangers fan who lived the dream and went on to be named the Greatest Ever Ranger.

What was he like as a teammate? Greigy was the first you would turn to in the trenches. He demanded, expected, the best out of everyone and he got it. I don't think I saw him lose many fifty-fifty balls and his battling qualities set the tone for so many of our greatest wins.

There is a bit of a myth that Greigy was just a hard man but he could play. He could spray passes around and he also got a goal now and then.

It was an honour to play alongside him. He was a tremendous player for every one of his seventeen years.

ALEX MACDONALD

Alex was massive Rangers fan as a boy. Even now, when you meet him at functions, his love for the club just bursts out of him. He was your original box-to-box midfielder – a blindside nightmare for opposing defences, fuelled by the amazing engine of a genuine fitness fanatic.

For a wee guy, Doddie was one of the best headers of a ball I've ever seen. He also had the heart of a lion and would get stuck in to guys twice his size. Without doubt, he is one player who could easily have made the transition from his own time to the demands of the modern game.

WILLIE JOHNSTON

I loved Bud – as a player and also as a pal. Sure, he had his moments, such as at the World Cup in 1978 or the madness that overtook him at times when he took exception to being kicked by an opposition defender but, in terms of his ability, wee Bud was right up there. Equally comfortable with either foot, his dribbling could mesmerise defenders and he would whip in crosses at electric pace and, like Doddie, he was another wee guy who was great in the air.

He served Rangers and Scotland with equal distinction and weighed in with crucial goals, most notably on the run-up to Barcelona and then in the final itself. For a striker, it was a dream to have Bud on one flank and Coop on the other.

GORDON SMITH

Pretty Boy Smithy was the only guy I ever played with who could go out on a rain-soaked mud-heap of a pitch and come back in with not a hair out of place or a splatter of dirt on his shorts. He glided across the pitch and he was a very, very good player at Rangers.

An intelligent player who could make runs into the channels and drift off defenders, Smithy would be best playing just off the front two. I formed a superb partnership with him in 1978 and I think we scored more than fifty goals that season.

He was brave, knew the way to goal and was another who maybe didn't get the praise at Rangers that some of his performances merited. In saying that, sometimes, when I hear him on the radio and TV, I wonder if he ever listened to anything I tried to teach him about the game!

At the time of writing he has just been asked to fill Scotland's hottest seat, as chief executive of the SFA. Good luck, Smithy!

DEREK JOHNSTONE

I've had to put myself in there at centre forward. People have asked me many times what my favoured position was and I did enjoy it up front – I started off as a striker and I loved scoring goals. I was never the quickest across the deck but my strengths were holding up the ball and winning things in the air. The way I have lined up this team, with two wide players, I think it would be important to have a target man and I feel that was my best role.

Looking back at my record of 210 goals for Rangers, I think that measures up fairly well, considering I did play a lot of the time in defence and even in midfield. Who knows how many I would have scored had I been a striker throughout my career but I'd like to think it would have been well over the 250 mark.

COLIN STEIN

We called him Louis, after the Louisville Lip, the nickname of Cassius Clay, later Muhammad Ali. Like the great fighter, Steiny had the gift of the gab. He was *the* man. What a tremendous Rangers striker! He was a legend to play alongside.

When I joined Rangers, he was the player I looked up to and I learned a lot from him. He has one of those infectious personalities and was a real bubbly character in the dressing room. On the pitch, he was immense. He had the knack of being able to hang in the air and he won a lot of headers and scored a few goals through that skill.

Centre halves just hated playing against him. I think he got his career at Rangers off to an amazing start with eight goals in three games. He was quite simply a star.

JOCK WALLACE – MANAGER

Big Jock – I smile and shut my eyes at the very mention of his name, despite having been on the receiving end of more of his infamous slaps than most. Jock was one of the finest managers Scotland has produced. He was a real Rangers man and, as I say elsewhere, it broke his heart to go. When he went to Leicester City, the first thing he would do after a game was charge into the dressing room and get the TV on to find out the Rangers score.

Jock had amazing success at Rangers in the 70s, ending Celtic's dominance and their bid for ten titles in a row. He took the team to two Trebles in three years – an incredible achievement – and he epitomised everything Rangers should be about.

Like every Rangers fan, it was hard for me to watch the club going into the decline it did after Jock left but then Graeme Souness arrived and transformed not only Rangers but the whole of Scottish football.

So that's the finest eleven from my time at Rangers. Souness, the man who started the big-name, highly paid influx into our game, figures prominently in my second eleven. Looking back over those twenty years or so at Rangers, it has again been extremely difficult to pick a team and again I'm sure many will disagree with my choices.

I would have loved to see my old boys take on this classy bunch. In the interests of fairness, they also line up in 3–4–3 formation. So, here they are – the best Rangers eleven I've seen since 1986:

Goram; Stevens, Gough, Butcher; Durrant, Gascoigne, Souness, Albertz; Laudrup, McCoist and Hateley

ANDY GORAM

Without question, Andy was the finest goalie ever to wear the keeper's jersey at Rangers. People talk about goalies being worth maybe ten points a season to their teams. Well, I would say Andy Goram was worth at least fifteen points to Rangers. He was an unbelievable keeper who could pull off saves that defied gravity. You looked at Andy and wondered how he did it. He would come out for games with all that padding on the knees and look nothing like a top-flight keeper but his saves were incredible and he was a major reason for the success of that nine-in-a-row Rangers side.

When Tommy Burns was manager of Celtic, he said he had already picked out the words for his tombstone – 'Andy Goram broke my heart.' And he was right. How many Old Firm games did Goram win? 'The Goalie' was immense.

GARY STEVENS

The biggest compliment he can be paid is that Rangers have never replaced him. Fans still say that to me about the right-back role and I think they are bang on.

Stevens was a tremendous athlete who could get up and down the right flank all day but he was also very intelligent and very rarely got caught out – apart from that pass back in the Scottish Cup Final that allowed Aberdeen's wee Joe Miller to score. But that was just about the only blunder he made.

Stevens was also very good in the air and could provide great cover. He formed a great relationship with Trevor Steven and was, all in all, a class act.

RICHARD GOUGH

There have been few better centre halves than Goughie – he was a leader, an organiser and a competitor. He had everything in his game and turned out to be up there with the club's best captains.

Richard would attack everything in the air. He was also quick on the deck and a great reader of the game. He was fearless, hated losing and got the best out of every player alongside him.

His name will always be remembered as the skipper who took the club to nine titles – a defender every manager would have had in his team.

TERRY BUTCHER

Big Tel arrived at Rangers in 1986 as the club's first high-profile signing. He was captain of England and the first sign that Souness meant business.

I loved watching Terry. His attitude was superb. A bit like John Greig, he was very gritty and a fierce competitor who would motivate and lead by example. I can't forget that image of him with blood-soaked bandages on his head and that was exactly the way he played. He would put his head in where it hurts and he brought a tremendous presence to the Rangers defence.

I have Terry in there as well for his threat in the opposition box. He could score goals from set-pieces and, on occasions, would come forward and pop in a long-distance effort with that left peg – just a tremendous player and captain.

IAN DURRANT

Durranty was breaking into the Rangers team when I arrived for my second spell. I sensed he was a special talent and, in terms of natural ability, I don't think there have been many better. What a shame he was cut down by that shocking Neil Simpson challenge. I don't think the wee man ever scaled the same heights after that dreadful day at Aberdeen, even though he did return to the Rangers team and scored a few crucial goals.

Durrant was special. He was so clever on the ball and could see things before other people. He was a superb finisher, often ending his trademark delayed runs into the box with a super goal.

Souness said he thought Durrant could have gone abroad and been huge and I agree – he was one of the best players Rangers have ever had.

PAUL GASCOIGNE

Gascoigne was a genius. The lad had his mad moments and he was never far from the front pages (who wasn't?) but he was at his most content on a football field – and, boy, could he play. Gazza was an entertainer, a maverick, and he was blessed with sublime skills that were a joy to behold.

Having had so many injury problems, I wondered if he could scale the heights when Walter Smith signed him from Lazio but, in my opinion, Gazza was at his very best when he played for Rangers. Maybe that was because he was playing in a league that was easier for him to dominate but, over that period of almost three years when he was at Ibrox, his contribution was magnificent. He scored crucial goals, set up plenty for the team and produced those moments you'll never forget – like the hat-trick against Aberdeen that clinched eight titles in a row.

Some have said he could have made the difference in the

failed bid for ten titles and that it had been a mistake to sell him to Middlesbrough. But I think Rangers got the best out of Paul and he will always be loved by the fans.

GRAEME SOUNESS

Souness was a born winner. I love the stories about him being on the losing side in a Cup Final and how he would come back to the dressing room and throw his runners-up medal in the bin. 'I don't collect them!' he would say.

I had the pleasure of playing with Graeme a few times in the national side and I have seldom come across a player with such desire and will to win. He was a real hard man as several midfielders found out to their cost. And even if, from time to time, he did perhaps put his foot in after the ball had gone, there is not a manager in the game who would not take a Souness in their team.

He could pick a pass and score goals plus he was an all-rounder who inspired those around him. He had the same attitude as a manager as he did as a player. If you didn't buy into Graeme's way of playing, you were out. He was just one of the best Scottish players of any generation.

JORG ALBERTZ

The big German had many things in his locker but his main asset was goals. Ask any Rangers fan about 'The Hammer' and they will rhyme off all the crackers he banged in for the club.

I'll never forget when Rangers played Celtic two weeks in a row, once in the Scottish Cup semi-final at Parkhead and then in the league at Ibrox, and he scored almost identical goals in both games. Running from the halfway line, he went past Celtic defenders and then slammed the ball into the net.

I think he averaged about fourteen goals a season from midfield, which is impressive and invaluable. I know Jorg's work rate wasn't the best and that's why he fell foul of Dick Advocaat. He didn't like to track back but I always felt he was a tremendous midfielder and he has to be out there on the left side for me.

It was a shame he left Rangers when he did after his fall-out with Advocaat. He loved the club and I think he would have ended his career at Ibrox had he been given that opportunity.

BRIAN LAUDRUP

World-class is an overused plaudit but there is no other way to describe the Dane. He arrived at Ibrox in 1994 and quickly became one of the finest players ever seen at the club. His brother Michael was always the one with the massive reputation but Brian had as much quality.

He shone in Scottish football and he made it look so easy. At times, he was on a different planet – not only to the hapless defenders he faced but also to many of his teammates. Brian could dribble past fullbacks and he could easily outpace the quickest players. And he was also great at cutting inside.

The first time I met him, I could not believe with how tall he was. He was well over 6ft and, for such a big guy, his speed, movement and balance were unbelievable. The thing I liked about Laudrup was that he took as much enjoyment out of setting up goals as he did scoring them. If you look back at the videos, you'll see he was the one player who would always square a ball across goal, rather than go for glory himself if he felt a teammate was in a better position than he was.

There's a debate who, between Brian Laudrup and Henrik

Larsson, was the best foreign player the Scottish game has ever seen. It's a hard call to make but Brian had only four years here while Henrik had double that so it's not a level playing field.

Like Albertz, I think he left Rangers too early and, unfortunately, it never worked out for him at Chelsea or Ajax.

ALLY McCOIST

What can I say? Coisty's was the first name on my team-sheet for this eleven. He was the finest goalscorer Rangers have ever had and he's a great guy into the bargain. His goals record speaks for itself but there was a lot more to Coisty than just finding the back of the net.

The fans were slow to accept him and people didn't give his all-around game the credit it deserved. Yes, the goals were there but he made a few as well and he also worked tirelessly for the team. He was a poacher but he was a team player too and he hated losing, even in training matches. You could not put a price on Ally McCoist in the modern game.

It is no surprise he is now back at the club in a managerial capacity. A legend, Ally loves Rangers.

MARK HATELEY

Hateley was a powerhouse of a centre forward. He would batter into a centre half as early as he could, just to set the tone. He bullied defenders and earned a fearsome reputation for his aggression. For all that he was big and strong, Mark had tremendous speed across the deck, which is unusual for a big lad.

He had a good touch too and could hold the ball up, which was perfect for small, nippy strikers as he would provide them with so many flick-ons.

He had a tough start from the fans at Ibrox but he showed great strength of character to fight back and become one of their heroes. Of course, his Ibrox double against Aberdeen when Rangers clinched the title did help! After that, he banged in plenty of goals and went from strength to strength.

Walter Smith brought him back from QPR when Rangers were going for nine titles in a row but he wasn't the same player. However, in his first Old Firm game at Parkhead, his mere presence on the pitch caused panic. He played a part in the only goal scored that day as Rangers won 1–0 and then he got sent off but he was a tremendous servant to the club.

WALTER SMITH – MANAGER

It was no contest. Dick Advocaat and Alex McLeish had great success at the club but the man who led Rangers to their nine-in-a-row has to be the boss.

Walter was a Rangers fan all his life and, in 1986, he jumped at the chance to join Graeme Souness on the coaching side. Those five years as number two served him well and, when he took over after Graeme left for Liverpool, he came into his own. He won trophy after trophy and made Rangers the dominant force in the land. Maybe the European results and performances could have been better but the quest for nine titles in a row dominated everything and he got Rangers there. Although Smith fell just short of ten, his record is immense. And it was hardly a major surprise when he came back to replace Paul Le Guen in January 2007.

So there they are – DJ's Greatest Rangers Teams. But which one would come out on top? Well, there would have been some titanic battles all over the field and I don't think there would have been many goals in it but I would go for my team winning 2–1. And the winner? A Derek Johnstone header at the back stick after I get in between Gough and Butcher to head home a Bud Johnston cross!

20

GREATEST EVER HURT

Rangers Football Club has been on the go since 1873 and, during that time, it has produced countless footballers of genuine quality. In 1999, Rangers supporters had been asked to vote for the players they thought most merited inclusion in the Greatest Ever Rangers Team and a packed audience attended the dinner and presentation ceremony held to mark the occasion when eleven men would receive the mark of distinction of being included in this team. The names were called out and, one by one, eleven legendary men answering to those names headed for the stage as those watching witnessed the Greatest Ever Rangers Team being pieced together. To find yourself in such company would be the ultimate honour.

Since that evening, people have asked me many times whether or not I knew beforehand if I was going to be in the team. The truth is I had no idea whether I had been chosen or not. The results were kept from everyone apart from the committee and I just sat there and sweated with the rest. There were some nailed-on certainties who were bound to be in the Greatest Ever Rangers Team but some places were very much up for debate. I never counted myself as one of the certainties but I prayed that my name would still be called.

From The Goalie, Andy Goram, through the defence and

midfield they came – heroes all. Then it was down to naming the two strikers – well, one striker actually as the other was always going to be Ally McCoist. No one could argue against Coisty being the finest striker the club has ever had. Even though I had played many matches for Rangers in defence – as well as quite a few in midfield – I always felt my best chance of securing a place in this team of stars would be as McCoist's partner upfront.

I laugh sometimes when Coisty says he idolised me and the likes of Colin Stein. If I was setting out in the game now or if I had a young son who wanted to see how it's done, I'd get a McCoist DVD on. He was genuine world class.

I've never talked publicly about how absolutely gutted I was that night when Mark Hateley was named in the side as the other striker although those close to me saw how hurt I was.

He went up to complete the Greatest Ever Rangers Team. The eleven chosen by the fans were:

ANDY GORAM, SANDY JARDINE, TERRY BUTCHER, RICHARD GOUGH, JOHN GREIG, DAVIE COOPER, PAUL GASCOIGNE, JIM BAXTER, BRIAN LAUDRUP, ALLY MCCOIST AND MARK HATELEY

I've nothing against big Mark who I like a lot – we have worked together since on Radio Clyde and get on well – but I can't lie and say that I wasn't hurt by my exclusion in his favour. I played 546 games for Rangers, scoring 210 goals, and I felt that achievement would have edged me ahead of someone who had played 218 games and scored half the goals I did.

Now I am not taking anything away from big Mark. He was a wonderful striker for Rangers and many times I've sat and enthused over his commitment, skill and desire for the club.

He was a big, strong front man and I know that the fans took him to their hearts after he scored that double to clinch the league against Aberdeen in 1991. But, if you are looking at length of service – and contribution – then I felt I had a good case. I can't deny that I was very upset that night. I stayed and tried to enjoy the rest of my night after the disappointment but it took a while for it to sink in.

There were a number of schools of thought about why I wasn't selected by the fans but, for me, it was purely a generation thing. Most of the voting was done on the internet and through the *Rangers News*. Look at the team that was picked. Only four of those players – Jardine, Greig, Baxter and Cooper – played during the 70s or before. The rest were all modern-day guys and I think the average age of those who voted must have counted heavily. It's understandable that most of the people who voted probably did so on the evidence of players they had actually seen in the flesh. Most of the voters were probably in short trousers when I was out there playing for Rangers! No matter, it did hurt me a lot. I just didn't think there was any way you could compare the service I had given Rangers to that of big Mark – again with all due respect to him.

There were many other players who could have felt the way I did on the night. Afterwards, I spoke to the comedian and entertainer wee Andy Cameron, one of the most ardent Rangers fans you'll ever meet. His favourite player was Jimmy Millar, and he put forward a strong case for him being in the team. Again, how many of those who voted had actually seen Jimmy play?

There were, no doubt, many more who would have come into that category. I know it's all about opinions and I'm sure that the same thing happened when Celtic had their Greatest

Ever Team awards a few years later. There were probably some fantastic Celtic players sitting in the room wondering why they hadn't been chosen. It was one of the biggest disappointments of my life but, later on, I was inducted into the Rangers Hall of Fame and that was a very proud moment for me. It felt incredibly rewarding to be in there, alongside the best players to have pulled on a blue jersey.

When you go up the famous marble staircase at Ibrox, there is a huge board that dominates the wall. On it are the names of all the players voted into the Hall of Fame. Although it's nice that my name is up there, it would, of course, have been even nicer if it had been in the top team too.

I go into Murray Park for a press conference on Fridays and I go in through the Youth Reception. On the wall right at the doors as you head into the corridor that takes you into the main building is a very good oil painting of all the players chosen in the Greatest Ever Rangers Team. They have been painted wearing the home strip from the particular time they played. It's very special. I always have a glance at it and think that I should have been there.

21

TRUE BLUE

So just where do I feel I stand now in the eyes of the Rangers fans? I am aware that some of them don't like me, especially an element of the younger support. They hear me on the radio criticising the team and feel that, as I was a Rangers player for so many years, I shouldn't be doing it. But sometimes they are told things that I am 'supposed' to have said and a bit of a bandwagon starts. I am well aware that I get a lot of stick on some fans' internet chat-rooms and they seem to think of me as some kind of Rangers' lackey. That is just nonsense but, on occasions, some people only listen to what they want to hear.

The Rangers fans are probably the most critical in this country. When a former player starts to have a go at the things that are going on, they'll turn on him and say he shouldn't be doing it as he played for the club. But I just give an honest opinion on Rangers. That's my job and I will always call it as I see it at the time. If that upsets an element of the fans, there is nothing I can do about it. But for them to say that I am disloyal to Rangers or that I have turned my back on the club that I was part of for fifteen years is just not true and really quite hurtful.

I would say that the older generation maybe thinks more of me. Maybe they remember what I did on the pitch more than what I say on the radio or write in my newspaper column now.

And I think many of these supporters recall the way I was at the club. Rangers was all I knew. It was my life from not long after I was out of short trousers! When I first broke into the team after the 1970 Cup Final, there was not a player who was invited to more supporters' functions around the country than I was. On Saturdays, even after games, I would sometimes go to two or three fans' presentations a night. And I didn't do it as a chore, like some players do these days, I did it because I wanted to be amongst the Rangers fans. They were like my second family.

I think that is a major problem nowadays. You rarely get any kind of affinity between players and the fans. I think that Rangers should insist that their players go to far more supporters' clubs functions – they should be out there amongst the fans.

I know that I do take a fair bit of stick – but I am a Rangers fan. I always will be. And I always want the team to do well. Do the people who have a go at me honestly think that I sit there and want the club not to do well? I went through some very barren times at Rangers as a player and I know how the dark times feel.

So it did annoy me when the club were in free-fall over the past couple of seasons. I enjoyed the two last day title successes in 2003 and 2005 as much as the next fan. Those were amazing moments but recently those days have been too few and far between. For Rangers not to be challenging Celtic is just not good enough.

Unfortunately two managers, Alex McLeish and Paul Le Guen, paid the price for a lack of success with their jobs. I like big Alex a lot and we always get on well. He did a great job at Rangers under severe restrictions when he wasn't given enough money to spend but he still managed to win seven trophies against Martin O'Neill's Celtic. Then Le Guen arrived and everyone bought into what he would do but it was a shambles and I was not surprised that he lasted just six months.

For me, the only man able to turn things around was Walter Smith. Rangers could not afford to take any more gambles and he has the club in his blood. Nothing would give me more pleasure than to see him and my close pal Ally McCoist, along with Kenny McDowall, restore Rangers to the number-one team in Glasgow. But it will be hard for them at the moment as Celtic are a strong side.

I will never shirk from giving an opinion on Rangers but some fans seem to think that I get fed the party line from the club and the chairman. Of course I speak to people inside Rangers and I have always enjoyed a decent relationship with Sir David Murray but we have had disagreements and to suggest I am just some kind of media puppet for the club is a complete joke.

I do believe that the majority of Rangers fans still respect what I did for the club. I gave *everything* I had to Rangers and took the kicks and bruises along the way. My loyalty to the club cost me a lot of money and I had to skipper them through some hellish times.

In the face of the kind of stick I take, it was quite humbling for me when I had a tribute dinner early in 2007. For a number of years, I had been reluctant to go with the idea despite being approached about it a few times. But then a number of Glasgow businessmen pushed it as they felt I deserved a night because of the service I'd given to the club.

The dinner sold out in a couple of weeks. Around 900 people turned out and it was an emotional night for me. I was so glad that the charities benefited and it also proved to me that I still had a place in the hearts of the Rangers fans. OK, maybe not all of them – but a fair few turned out that night and that meant a lot. And, whenever I go on trips abroad, I still get fans coming up to me and asking for a picture or an autograph. And that is something I'll always enjoy. So, to those who have a dig at me, I say this – I am only doing my job and I give my honest opinion so please don't ever say that I don't care about Rangers or that I don't want them to win because that is just utter nonsense.

I totally understood where big Dado Prso was coming from back in May 2007, when he was in tears leaving the pitch at Ibrox. Here was a guy who had only been at the club for three years yet, in that short time, he had been bitten by the Rangers bug. He was so emotional about leaving and that is the way the club can affect you. I felt exactly the same all those years ago when I walked out the door for the last time. Rangers was the thing that made me and I gave the club everything I had in return. And I look back with immense pride at what I achieved.

When I was sitting up there at the tribute dinner back in February 2007, a lot went through my mind. In front of me were the two tables where my kids and brothers were seated. I also had a lot of friends there. I looked around and it was quite emotional. I thought about all the things I'd seen in my life, all the mistakes I'd made, the highs and lows and even the scares I'd had with my own health. Inside, I felt content that I'd managed to build bridges with my children and we were fine. I felt happier inside myself because I had addressed my health issues, lost weight and felt good about myself again.

My life is good, I thought. I am healthy, I am still in the public eye with my media work and I'll continue to enjoy that and not shy away from saying how I feel. And when they showed the videos of me on the big screens scoring some of my proudest goals, I had a lump in my throat. That was me! That was the place I'd always felt was home – out on the pitch in a Rangers jersey – and the club will always be in my heart.

When I die, I am going to have some things from my time at Rangers in my coffin with me. I won't take the Cup Winners' Cup medal that hangs around my neck every day – that will be passed on to my kids – but I'll have a scarf that I've kept from a while back and one or two pictures plus some other things that I'll keep private. That is the way I want to go.

I'd like to hope that people will look back in the years ahead and see me not just as Derek Johnstone but Derek Johnstone of Rangers.

DEREK JOHNSTONE:

STATISTICS

Born:	Dundee, 4 November 1953

1970–1983	Rangers FC
1983–Jan 1985	Chelsea FC
Oct 83–Nov 83	Dundee United FC (loan)
Jan 1985–1986	Rangers FC
1986–1987	Partick Thistle FC
	(player-manager)

Honours

1 European Cup Winners' Cup

3 Scottish League Championships

5 Scottish Cups

5 Scottish League Cups

1 English Second Division Championship

1978 Scottish PFA Player of the Year

1978 Scottish Football Writers' Player of the Year

Season	Appearances	(Sub)	Goals
RANGERS FC			
1970/71:	14	(7)	8
1971/72:	34	(1)	12
1972/73:	47		10
1973/74:	43	(1)	2
1974/75:	35		16
1975/76:	50	(1)	31
1976/77:	42		21
1977/78:	47		39
1978/79:	52	(1)	16
1979/80:	45	(2)	21
1980/81:	33	(4)	7
1981/82:	39	(3)	16
1982/83:	26		11
CHELSEA FC			
1983/84:	2		0
1984/Jan 85:	2		0
DUNDEE UNITED FC			
Oct 83–Nov 83:	4		3
RANGERS FC			
Jan 85–May 85:	12		1
1985/86:	10	(1)	0
PARTICK THISTLE FC			
1986/87:	4		0
TOTAL	562 appearances		214 goals

DEREK JOHNSTONE: STATISTICS

International Career

Caps	14
Won	5
Drawn	3
Lost	6
Goals	2

Date	Result
12.05.73	Wales 0 – Scotland 2
16.05.73	Scotland 1 – Northern Ireland 2
19.05.73	England 1 – Scotland 0
22.06.73	Switzerland 1 – Scotland 0
30.06.73	Scotland 0 – Brazil 1
30.10.74	Scotland 3 – East Germany 0
16.04.75	Sweden 1 – Scotland 1
07.04.76	Scotland 1 – Switzerland 0
08.05.76	Scotland 3 – Northern Ireland 0
15.05.76	Scotland 2 – England 1
22.02.78	Scotland 2 – Bulgaria 1
13.05.78	Scotland 1 – Northern Ireland 1
17.05.78	Scotland 1 – Wales 1
19.12.79	Scotland 1 – Belgium 3